Books of Light

To All Who Write,
And As They Write,
Bring In New Light
For Us To See By

Books of Light

A Compilation of Reviews
of Outstanding Books in the Fields
of Science Fiction, Metaphysics,
Holistic Health, and the Esoteric

by the Editors of Books of Light Book Club

ARIEL PRESS
Columbus, Ohio

Second Edition

This book is made possible by gifts
to the Publications Fund of Light

Books of Light
Copyright © 1986, 1988 by Light

All Rights Reserved. No part of this book may be used
or reproduced in any manner whatever without written permission, except in the case of brief quotations
embodied in articles and reviews. Printed in the United
States of America. Direct inquiries to: Ariel Press, 3854
Mason Road, Canal Winchester, Ohio 43110.

ISBN 0-89804-049-3

Preface

This little book is meant to be a doorway into a new dimension. It is a collection of reviews of books that are featured in the Books of Light book club. Reading these reviews is not the same as reading the books themselves. But if you read one of these reviews and are inspired to read the book, then you have opened the door and passed into the next dimension.

It is a very special dimension, too, filled with magic and mystery, love and goodwill, joy and laughter, adventure and triumph, struggle and growth, wisdom and insight. It is a dimension that will stretch your mind and exercise your imagination. It will open up new mental horizons, and reveal new possibilities you have never dreamed of before. It will challenge your self-honesty, and if you pass the test, it will lay the groundwork for real transformation and genuine spiritual growth.

This is an inner dimension, reached by reading and thinking. But not by reading any old book. The books reviewed in this small volume have all been chosen because of their unusual capacity to introduce us to some facet of our inner life and potential to grow.

Books of Light is a special kind of book club. The titles we feature must radiate the light of intelligence, or we do not select them. To qualify for our club, a book must help us, one way or another, become more aware of the inner potential of our humanity and show us what to do with it. This is no small order. Many writers claim to be inspired, but their words lack light. It is rare to find a writer who truly is inspired by his or her inner self, the inner dimensions of life. When we do find such writers, we should celebrate their talent and applaud their accomplishments. This is the purpose of this collection. It is not a collection of *critiques*, but of *reviews*. It praises creativity and genius, instead of finding fault with it. It is meant to open doors.

This book contains reviews of both fiction and nonfiction. The fiction tends to be mostly fantasy and science fiction, although there are some outstanding exceptions to this general rule—the novels of Joan Grant, Taylor Caldwell, Charles Williams, and Dion Fortune, to name a few. Many people shy away from fiction, because they think "it's not true." This is a tragic misunderstanding. Good fiction often reveals and describes to us the nature of the inner dimensions of life far more powerfully than any stuffy treatise. In fact, many of the novels chosen for review in this collection are veritable textbooks on one aspect of the inner life or another. Colin Wilson's *The Mind Parasites*, for instance, gives a far more lucid account of psychic attack than any nonfiction book. Ursula LeGuin's masterpiece, *The Earthsea Trilogy*, tells us far more about the process of overcoming the dark elements within ourselves—and radiates more light in the process—than almost any book on metaphysics or personal transformation. Certainly Anne McCaffrey's

Dragonriders of Pern series teaches us more about the true workings of the subconscious than any college text on psychology!

The nonfiction that we feature embraces many categories, from holistic healing to psychic phenomena, from metaphysics to meditation, from autobiography to the arcane, and from the creative to the cosmic. Nonfiction titles range from *The I Ching Workbook* to *The Masterthinker's Handbook*, from *Active Meditation* to *Practical Mysticism*, from *The New View Over Atlantis* to *The Destiny of America*. We do not promote any enshrined viewpoint in choosing these titles, save one. Each book must lead us to a greater understanding and awareness of light—the light within us.

What is this light? Answering this question is part of the fun and adventure of reading these books. In brief, however, we can state that it is the light within great ideas—the light which inspires these authors to write their books, and the light which fills us with new ideas and fresh insights as we read them. In a magical way, reading is meant to be an act of sharing and communion, as we interact with the same ideas and inner realities which first inspired the book.

The perceptive reader will quickly discover what this means. Something alchemical occurs as we read these books. They inspire us to new aspiration and new achievement. They enrich our thinking. There is a living presence in each of these books, and as we interact with this living presence, new doors in consciousness open to us, awaiting our exploration.

Our intent is to help you open some of these doors. In no way do we mean to suggest that the following set of reviews is a complete bibliography of the best books in these fields. Such a list would be almost impossible to compile. So we have imposed a few limitations. First, all of these books are presently in print. We have purposefully excluded out of print books, no matter how inspired, simply because a book which cannot be read cannot open any doors!

The second limitation is an even more practical one. We have only included books we have actually featured in the book club. There are many excellent books which will be selected as the club continues to serve its members; these books will be included in future editions. C.W. Leadbeater was represented in the first edition of this collection, for instance, only by his book *Thought-Forms*, even though he is one of our favorite authors. In this new edition, several of his books are reviewed. What made the difference? Quite simply, the books became available again. At the same time, some books included in the first edition have been dropped from this one.

Undoubtedly, there will be many people who take exception with our choices. They will wonder why specific authors are not included, especially if they have found them particularly inspirational. "Just what is your criteria for including and excluding books?" they will demand. This is an unanswerable question, for we have no formula, except that a book radiate light. But there are some types of books which we *do not* and *will not* promote:

• Those which espouse the use of drugs as a means to the expansion of consciousness or enlightenment. No matter how fascinating these accounts might be, they do not lead us toward the light. They promote only silliness and irresponsibility.

- The "wow wonderful" type of book, in which the author suddenly discovers proof of life after death, reincarnation, or psychic communication. Such books play an important role, of course, but all of these phenomena have been documented so many times in the past that the "new revelation" begins to tire, except for people who have never considered such ideas before. In selecting our titles, we assume that our members have some acquaintance with these ideas and want to be stimulated by important new thoughts, not just convinced of their integrity and truthfulness.

- The "wow wonderful" type of book by celebrities. Famous people are often very helpful in spreading exotic ideas and making the average person more comfortable with them. But just having a famous name does not make anyone more enlightened, or more knowledgeable, than anyone else.

- Books capitalizing on popular fads. Enlightenment is measured neither by popularity nor by current fashion. We do not think we really need another book on how to jog your way to nirvana, how to become clairvoyant while you sleep, or how the Chernobyl disaster was caused by the misapplication of psychic energy by secret Russian mediums. If we wanted to be amused in this way, we would rather watch an old Marx brothers' movie.

- Imitations. Imitation is undoubtedly the sincerest form of flattery, but it is not usually worth much. Unfortunately, the fields of metaphysics and psychic discovery are flooded by cheap imitations. There are, for example, at least a dozen books out on color therapy, yet none compare with the very first ones written on the subject by S.G.J. Ouseley. That is why we feature his books, not the imitations. Recently, the market has also been flooded with books about the esoteric impact of music. Yet none come close to equaling Cyril Scott's book on the subject, *Music, Its Secret Influence Throughout the Ages*. So that is the one we carry.

• Wolves in sheep's clothing. Many books are written which claim to deal with holistic healing or psychic discoveries, yet fail to reveal anything genuine of the inner life. Instead, their treatment is very superficial, and their recommendations are highly influenced by materialistic assumptions. A good example of this is any book which recommends vegetarianism as a spiritual practice. It is what we feed our minds and inner self that determine our progress toward enlightenment, not what we feed our physical bodies. No one yet has ever eaten his or her way to heaven.

In short, we have made a conscious effort to sift through and discard the cheap, the shabby, and the phony. Each of the books reviewed in this volume is a treasure. There are no ringers.

Yet many people will pick up these treasures and fail to recognize them for what they are. No doors will open. They will not tap the light within the words. They may even dismiss the words as "silly" or "impractical" or "nonsense."

How can this happen? It can happen because there is an art to reading inspired literature, be it fiction or nonfiction. It is not enough just to read the words; we must also try to read the thoughts behind the words—the light or creative idea which originally inspired the author. Reading is meant to be an act of transcendence, where the power of the words lifts us up to a higher level of perception than we normally enjoy. But this can only happen if we are making the effort to read intelligently.

In reading nonfiction, we should do more than just try to absorb new facts. Filling our mind with facts prepares us only for trivia contests and cocktail parties. Facts have their place, but they are just the outer flesh of the inner idea. In reading, therefore, we must try to understand the basic ideas, not just facts. Even more importantly, we must take the most significant of these ideas and integrate them into our values, ethics, attitudes, goals, and character.

Reading about reincarnation is a good example of this principle. The average person loves to read about the vivid details of earlier lives of specific people, for this sets in motion speculation about his or her own previous lives, leading quickly to glamorous fantasies and unrealistic play-acting. None of this is productive thinking. The intelligent person, by contrast, will try to use the facts and examples of reincarnation that he or she reads about to stimulate mature contemplation about the archetypal processes of rebirth, accountability, and transformation. In this way, the magical act of reading opens up new doors—not just alluring blind alleys.

In reading fiction, we should do more than just escape into an absorbing story. Inspired fiction is usually highly symbolic; the plot unfolds on several levels all at once. There is the literal level of the story line, but there is also the hidden level of esoteric symbolism. The novel *Glory Road* by Robert Heinlein is a good example of this. On the literal level, it may seem to some people to be little more than a somewhat gory adventure story spiced with sex. Symbolically, however, a wholly different story unfolds, as we see the adventures of the hero as the struggles of the aspirant on the spiritual path. There is great wisdom in this novel, yet the average reader might easily read the whole novel without grasping its insights and meanings at all.

These books demand that we stretch our thinking and imagination. If we are satisfied with what we know already, these books will offend us. But if we hunger for more insight into life, these books will nourish us. They will nurture us with light.

No one's life ever needs to be dull, one-dimensional. The rich treasures of inspired reading are available to us all, if only we will avail ourselves of them. Whether you are new to the world of enlightened books, or a confirmed student of the arcane, the treasure awaits.

Acquiring These Books

Many of these books are readily available in most large bookstores; some will be easily found in libraries as well. This is especially true of the science fiction and popular fiction. But a substantial number of the books reviewed in this volume are not widely distributed and can be quite hard to find. Perhaps the appearance of this bibliography will inspire more stores and libraries to add these titles.

As this book goes to press, however, all of these books are presently in print and are available through Books of Light. Books of Light is a book club with a difference. It makes available a wide selection of inspired books, always at discounted prices, yet members are never under any pressure to purchase books. No books are ever sent automatically; only those which members specifically order are sent.

For current prices and availability of any of these books, just write to Books of Light, 3854 Mason Road, Canal Winchester, Ohio 43110. Or call toll free: 1-800-336-7769.

Books of Light

The I Ching Workbook
by R.L. Wing

The I Ching is an ancient Chinese philosophical and occult system with a rich and extensive tradition in successful use. It has been known in the West for many years, but most books on the subject have been unusually obtuse and hard to follow.

An excellent new book, *The I Ching Workbook* by R.L. Wing, remedies this problem. It is lucid, well-organized, and thoughtful—and is written for both the beginner and the expert. The beginner is able to start using the I Ching after just a few hours' reading. The expert will find *The I Ching Workbook* a provocative new approach to ancient ideas.

The I Ching is a mantic device which can be used to help make decisions and solve problems—but also to learn about and explore archetypal forces. It is a highly organized system of 64 archetypes, each represented by a "hexagram" of six lines, either broken or solid.

Hexagrams are determined by casting coins or sticks after formulating a specific question. Frequently, the resulting hexagram will change into a second one, thereby indicating the changing influences to be anticipated.

The value of the I Ching is that it is a remarkable aid for understanding the order of the universe and how universal forces influence mundane events. The ancient Chinese had an excellent grasp of the individual's place in the universe and saw archetypal forces reflected even in the smallest of events.

One of the significant features of the I Ching is that it

has never fallen into the hands of the ignorant. Many Western systems, such as astrology and the Tarot, were abandoned by intellectuals to gypsies and others. As a result, they have suffered grave indignities. The I Ching, by contrast, has always been held in high regard in China, and has been preserved and developed by the most intelligent of scholars. The Wing workbook maintains this tradition admirably.

Using the I Ching is really a miniature lesson in invoking the universe. Each use of it becomes a symbolic personification of archetypal forces. The I Ching forces the questioner to specify his request and then direct it to the oracle of the hexagrams.

It also forces the user to think intelligently about his or her question. The I Ching does not provide concrete answers to questions, but does delineate a short course in human psychology and the tides of human nature. If the questioner is willing to take the ideas and hints presented and think them through, much insight can be tapped.

In the *Workbook*, author Wing does an excellent job of helping the reader interpret each hexagram. A full page is given to examining the forces represented by each hexagram and suggesting ways these forces may work out. An adjoining page lists commentaries on the changing lines or conditions, and also provides the user with space to keep records and chart dominant themes. This allows the questioner to see the patterns which develop through repeated use of the I Ching— patterns that can tell us a great deal about our responsiveness to particular archetypal forces. Such patterns can represent invaluable clues to understanding recurring problems and the nature of our destiny.

For the purpose of this review, and to demonstrate how the I Ching works, the question "What is the value of using the I Ching?" was posed and the coins were tossed six times. The resulting hexagram was number 45 of the 64, called "Ts'ui" in Chinese and "Assembling" in English. The secondary or changing hexagram was number 25, called "Wu Wang" in Chinese and "Innocence" in English.

Upon consulting Wing's commentary on hexagram 45, it becomes clear that "assembling" refers to the gathering of universal forces; the I Ching is especially valuable in discerning these patterns and how they influence us. To quote the text: "By observing the way gatherings evolve, we can perceive the inner tendencies of heaven and earth and of all things. Within the Self, too, there is a central force of character that unifies thoughts and actions." These can be known through the study of the I Ching.

The second hexagram indicates the changes which can occur in one's life through the study of the I Ching. To quote the text: "The time demands an alignment with the flow of the cosmos. If you are a teacher, leader, or head of a family, use the insights and inspirations that will occur to fulfill the needs of those who rely on you. It is important to keep in mind that laws of the cosmos are divine and do not necessarily follow the desires of man."

The study of *The I Ching Workbook* by R.L. Wing is a fine introduction to the intelligent use of archetypal forces.

I Say Sunrise
by Talbot Mundy

"The world is visibly moving from bad to worse, if we can trust our senses. But can we trust senses that lie to us about such ordinary everyday occurrences as sunrise and sunset?"

Talbot Mundy says no, and encourages us to go *forward* to the beginning—the sunrise—of life, and awaken not our senses, but our consciousness. He challenges us to discover, and prove to ourselves, that joy *is* stronger than sorrow, love *is* stronger than hatred, hope *is* stronger than despair, energy *is* stronger than sloth, and good *is* stronger than evil.

I Say Sunrise is a joyous book, all the more remarkable because the joy that fills its pages was cultivated, the author reports, in the face of great struggle, shame, and grief. On the surface, *I Say Sunrise* is a statement of Talbot Mundy's philosophy of life, a metaphysical classic. But beneath the surface, it is more than this alone. It teaches us how to fill life with joy, so that we can triumph over struggle, shame, and grief, too.

It is also a direct assault on the limitations of mass consciousness, describing how the popular beliefs of society color the individual thinking of each of us, and what we can do to reclaim proprietorship over our own convictions and attitudes.

Along the way, there are chapters on death, reincarnation, the use of money, love, and prayer.

This is a powerful book; it awakens us from sleep. As Mundy writes: "What is beyond the darkness? Some say chaos and darker night. I Say Sunrise."

The Reappearance of the Christ

by Alice A. Bailey

Ever since Jesus walked the earth and set forth His new teachings of peace and goodwill, men and women have longed for His return. Many have prophesied His return at a specific time and place, attracting the interest of others, only to be disappointed by the absence of a physical appearance. What we have often forgotten is that the Christ, which is spirit, has never left us; He has always been with us. Instead of cultivating a better rapport with the spiritual reality which is the Christ, we have hoped for the reappearance of the exact physical form of Jesus.

In *The Reappearance of the Christ*, Alice Bailey takes humanity to task for its failure to cultivate an ongoing relationship with the living Christ, falling instead into an almost useless worship of a crucified Jesus. She paints a fascinating picture of just how active the Christ has been, not only throughout the ages but more importantly in our modern age—working behind the scenes, to be sure, from the inner levels, but nonetheless as the most important influence on the evolution of humanity.

She then goes on to outline point by point the changes we need to make in our thinking and action to establish right rapport with the Christ and allow Him—and the Hierarchy as a whole—to reappear physically and interact openly with humanity.

The Reappearance of the Christ is one of the most readable and perhaps the most important of all the books Alice Bailey wrote. It is highly recommended.

Kinship With All Life
by J. Allen Boone

The human race does not inhabit the planet earth alone. We share it with many kingdoms of life. Yet we often have little appreciation for the value of these other kingdoms.

As a race, we desperately need a larger perspective on life. We need to cultivate a deeper reverence for all life, and see the kingdoms which inhabit the earth—animal, plant, and mineral—as worthy expressions of the One Creator.

J. Allen Boone's remarkable book, *Kinship with all Life*, is a charming introduction to the true meaning of reverence. It is the story of Boone's personal experiences with animals, how he learned to communicate with them, and the respect and love he has developed for them.

The principal figure of the book is Strongheart, a famous movie dog of his day. Asked to care for Strongheart while his trainers were away, Boone readily consented. However, he soon began having second thoughts, as Strongheart seemed far more capable of taking care of Boone than the other way around! As he got to know the famous dog, Boone marveled at his range of intelligence—and found he could communicate telepathically with him.

These experiences led Boone to explore contacts with other animals, too—rattlesnakes, ants, and "Freddie the Fly." His observations and insights make fascinating and entertaining reading, and put a unique and practical focus on the concept of reverence for life.

This book is a joy to read.

No One Hears But Him
by Taylor Caldwell

"For all the talk of 'love' there is in the world today
the fact remains that never has the world been so absolutely loveless, hard of heart, murderous, cruel,
rejecting, contemptuous, and indifferent. Never has
the heart of man been so faithless as the heart of
modern man, for all the babble of 'involvement' and
'concern for humanity.' "

Wanting to see this change, Taylor Caldwell has
written a novel of unusual power—a novel which can
help us make this change in ourselves. *No One Hears
But Him* is the story of a great sanctuary, located in a
park in a large city. In this sanctuary waits The Man
Who Listens. He waits for the angry, the hopeless, the
cynical, the bereaved, and the burdened to come and
tell Him their story, so they may be healed.

The Man Who Listens hears but does not speak.
But as these angry, hopeless people tell of their trou-
bles and rage, a powerful change begins to occur within them. Sometimes they hear a voice within them,
speaking quiet counsel; sometimes they have an inner
vision. In some cases, the change is not dramatic at
all. But they begin to understand themselves and
what they can do to take control of their lives, and
they leave the sanctuary uplifted, with fresh wisdom
and poise.

The Man Who Listens, of course, is the Christ—the
Christ within us who can speak to us and guide us, if
we will only listen. Few novels contain a greater
power for transformation than this one. It should be
read—and heeded—by all.

WINGED PHARAOH
by Joan Grant

Outstanding fiction always has the capacity to conjure a setting and a time, and make the reader feel that he or she is right there, absorbing the flavor of the surroundings and participating in the action. Few novels, however, succeed in doing this as well as Joan Grant's classic story of ancient Egypt, *Winged Pharaoh*.

First published in 1937 but difficult to obtain in recent years, *Winged Pharaoh* is something far greater than the usual stories of vanity and intrigue found in cheap romances about Egypt. Revolving around the story of a young princess who becomes an initiate of the occult teachings of the time and then a "winged Pharaoh" in the first dynasty of ancient Egypt, this is a glorious novel, an epic in enlightened living. It provides a masterful glimpse into an era and culture which has been all but lost to history.

Sekhet-a-ra is the daughter of the Pharaoh and destined to become, with her brother Neyah, co-ruler of Kam, as Egypt was called in those times. As a child, she develops a strong love for the teachings of the mystery schools, fascinated by the stories told her by her father and Ptah-kefer, the high priest.

While still young, Sekhet-a-ra, or Sekeeta, as she is usually called, begins having psychic experiences of her own and is recognized as one who will be, with proper training, a "winged Pharaoh"—a ruler and priest with clairvoyant powers. At the age of ten, she is sent to the temple school for rigorous training in esoteric knowledge and the development of her inner powers and awareness. Much of the book is devoted to describing this training and the nature of the mysteries. For the reader who is interested in the psychic aspects of life, the principles of intelligent living, and the natural unfoldment of the spiritual life, these passages hold great keys to understanding. Indeed, they are written with such clarity, detail, and living presence that it is quite reasonable to believe, as Joan Grant has stated, that her story was really a "far memory" and not a work of fiction at all—an actual recollection and reconstruction of life in ancient Egypt.

Sekeeta's training concludes with a detailed account of her four days of initiation, during which time she is out of her body and facing powerful tests of her will and discernment. She is then ready to handle the challenges of being priestess and Pharaoh.

It is not possible to read this book without being struck by the realization that the ancient Egyptians were often far wiser in their approach to life than we are in modern society. They viewed dreams, for example, as out-of-body experiences of learning or service, and Sekeeta is given training to remember her dreams more clearly. As she progresses, she also finds she can be taught by discarnate teachers as well as her physical ones.

Sekeeta learns the mysteries of life after death, too. "We are all travelers upon a long journey, as we pass through many countries. We may find gardens and tranquil rivers where for a time we are happy; yet in our hearts, we know we are exiles and long to return to our true home." The journey, of course, is the time spent on earth; the true home is the inner life of spirit.

The person who craves salacious accounts of the court life of the Pharaohs may be disappointed by this story. But for the intelligent reader, *Winged Pharaoh* is a rare delight, a rich introduction to the cosmology, culture, healing arts, and psychic life of Egypt.

Today, as the mysteries of life are being restored to earth, the hidden and esoteric practices of 'Kam' provide us with a clue of what is to come in our society, as spirit once more dominates our culture and thinking. What was known to only a few priests in Egypt may, one day, become common knowledge to the whole of science, for the good of mankind.

Winged Pharaoh is an important book.

Divine Healing of Mind & Body
by Murdo MacDonald-Bayne

"The world is still eating of the fruit of the Tree of Knowledge of Good and Evil, and only when mankind takes hold of the Tree of Life—the Christ within—will his salvation come."

Taking hold of the Christ within and learning to use its power to heal the mind and the body is the theme of one of our age's most remarkable books, a transcription of 14 lectures delivered by Jesus through Dr. Murdo MacDonald-Bayne during the year 1948.

At the start of each lecture, the power and intelligence of the Master would take control of the body of MacDonald-Bayne and speak flawlessly and without pause about a topic of spiritual growth.

But the mechanics of how these lectures were given are not nearly as important as the peace, love, and illumination of the words recorded in this book. For *Divine Healing of Mind and Body* stands by itself, without claims and affadavits, as a series of brilliant insights into human and divine nature, prayer, and faith.

This is the sort of book which we can open at random, and no matter what we read, come away inspired and refreshed. When read from cover to cover, however, the ideas in this book become a magical presence which fills our thinking and awareness with beauty, reverence, love, and new insights.

There is great power, intelligence, truth, and healing in this book. It is highly recommended to all who seek to know God and take hold of the Christ within.

Esoteric Philosophy of Love & Marriage

by Dion Fortune

The subjects of sexual love and marriage are important ones to most people, but are also subjects which have been shrouded in mystery, dogma, guilt, confusion, and rumor. The person seeking to honor the higher principles of life often struggles greatly with these issues, without satisfactory resolution.

This book by Dion Fortune is one of the best statements in print regarding sexual love and marriage. It seeks to put the many areas of confusion regarding these issues into an esoteric perspective. As such, it considers sex to be one of the energies of life and self-expression, no more or less divine than any other energy. Like all energies of life, it must be used with respect, purpose, and self-control, or it will go awry—but it *is* an important, healthy, and creative element of human life.

In order to develop fully this basic theme, Miss Fortune begins with a brief examination of the esoteric doctrine of energy and its manifestation in consciousness and matter. This short summary alone makes the book well worthwhile, but it is actually just an introduction to her real topics: the esoteric concept of sex, the ideal marriage, the interplay of male and female polarities, and the creative potentials arising from a balanced use of these energies.

Esoteric Philosophy of Love and Marriage is an important book. It is highly recommended to all who want to *understand* the principles of life more completely.

Narcissus & Goldmund
by Hermann Hesse

"The basic image in a good work of art is not a real, living figure, although it may inspire it. The basic image is not flesh and blood; it is mind. It is an image that has its home in the artist's soul."

Goldmund's words to his friend Narcissus touch the life force of this superb novel, quite possibly the greatest written by Hermann Hesse. For this is a story about human creativity—not in flesh and blood, but in the mind.

Narcissus is a medieval monk in a remote abbey. Goldmund comes to the abbey as a student. The two become friends, and Goldmund wants to be a monk like Narcissus. But Narcissus knows the cloistered life is not for his friend, and convinces him to find his life in the outer world.

So Goldmund leaves to search for happiness in the world, first through romantic trysts with women, and then later as a sculptor. From time to time, his path takes him back to the abbey and Narcissus, but he never settles down. He continues to wander, searching for the vision which drives him onward—the vision which will fulfill his sense of being.

The friendship between Narcissus and Goldmund is strikingly similar to the ideal relationship between the soul and the personality. Each gives of his nature to the other and is enriched in return—and it is Narcissus who lives on, after his friend has died, to sustain the creative vision Goldmund has discovered.

Few stories are as powerful and as poignant as *Narcissus and Goldmund*.

The Impersonal Life

Within each human being, there is a central divine essence which is the *real self.* Few of us recognize this inner self, however. Instead, we identify with our physical body, our thoughts and feelings, and with the events which happen to us. As long as this is so, we are trapped in a shallow, highly personal life. But if we begin to listen to the voice of the real self, and come to accept it as the genuine heart of our life, we can reclaim our true heritage as a child of God. We can tap the power of *the impersonal life.*

Detaching from the mundane focus of the personal life and learning to identify with the voice of spirit is the theme of many, many books, but none describe this fundamental process of the spiritual path as clearly and comprehensively as *The Impersonal Life.* Written by Joseph S. Benner but published anonymously—to emphasize its basic message—*The Impersonal Life* is truly a classic statement of the power and nature of spirit.

In short, easy-to-read chapters, each written as a direct communication from the reader's own real self to his personality, *The Impersonal Life* describes the basic conflicts of human living, how they are resolved, and how resolving them advances the impersonal life of God.

There are also a number of excellent chapters which comment on a variety of overblown fictions of the "spiritual life," such as soul mates and spirit guides.

The Impersonal Life is a marvelous stimulus to personal and spiritual growth. It is highly recommended to all who seek to be more responsive to the real self.

Active Meditation
The Western Tradition
by Robert R. Leichtman, M.D. & Carl Japikse

There are two major elements in human consciousness: the personality, which we use in daily self-expression, and the higher self, which most of us largely ignore. The price we pay for ignoring the higher self, however, is an enormous one. It means we live without the enlightenment, love, and strength of our higher self.

Meditation is a set of practices which help us bring the life and power of the higher self into expression in the daily activities of the personality. The regular use of meditation enriches consciousness, illumines the mind, increases self-discipline, stimulates creativity, and integrates the personality with the higher self. It helps the personality attain the full potential of its design.

Effective meditation has been a part of every significant spiritual tradition in human history—because there is no better way of establishing contact between the personality and our higher self. There is no better way of tapping the divine energies of love, wisdom, and strength. There is no better path to enlightenment.

And yet, not all systems of meditation lead to enlightenment. In many systems, the art of meditation has been trivialized. Instead of serving as a method for establishing and maintaining contact with the higher self, it has all too often become a simple process of relaxing or quieting the mind and body—or concentrating on a single thought or sound. Many people accept these practices as legitimate aspects of meditation, but they are not.

Active Meditation: The Western Tradition, by Dr. Robert R. Leichtman and Carl Japikse, puts the art of meditation back in focus. Almost encyclopedic in scope, it is a comprehensive examination of the tradition, purpose, potential, and techniques of meditation. More importantly, it is a masterful statement of the emerging Western tradition of personal and spiritual growth. It is a book which challenges, inspires, enlightens, and informs. In fact, it sets the standard for meditation in the new age.

From beginning to end, the tone set by Leichtman and Japikse emphasizes the practical nature of meditation. To them, the subjects of meditation and personal growth are inseparable—the work of meditation should always be connected with the development of a greater capacity to act wisely and creatively in the physical plane. They decry the excessive passiveness which has crept into many systems of meditation, presenting instead a strong case that meditation is most effective when it is *active*. They state that the active practice of meditation *is* the Western tradition.

Active Meditation: The Western Tradition is therefore something more than just a precise definition of the art of meditation. It is also a thorough commentary on personal and spiritual growth. In specific, the authors describe:

- What meditation is—and is not.
- How meditation accelerates personal and spiritual growth.
- The nature of the higher self.
- How to contact the higher self.

- The proper relationship between the higher self and the personality.
- The work of integration.
- The skills of meditation and how to use them.
- Seven specific techniques of Active Meditation, for establishing an enlightened self-image, defining values and goals, mental housecleaning, healing the emotions, invoking wisdom, solving problems, and creative self-discovery.
- Meditating to help others.
- Group meditations.
- The evolution of consciousness.
- Problems associated with meditating and how to overcome them.

They also take on the task of exposing some of the more worn-out "sacred cows" of meditation and spiritual growth, which they handle very delightfully in a series of interludes with the angel "Herman." These slightly mischievous exchanges keep the book from getting too top heavy, as so many books on spiritual growth do, yet help us see the limits of many of the old traditions.

Throughout the book, Leichtman and Japikse work to strip away the vagueness and obscurity often associated with meditation and personal growth and treat their subject with common sense, clarity, and good humor. The result is a book which obviously does contain the seeds of a new tradition.

Active Meditation is a book which is easy to read and understand—yet also a book which will spur advanced meditators onto new discoveries, new realizations. It deserves to be *the* standard manual or reference book for all meditators.

The Bach
Flower Remedies
by Edward Bach, M.D.

Dr. Edward Bach believed the heart of healing must be focused on the ills of the emotions—not physical distress. To him, the bodily ills are merely symptoms of far more serious problems—our fears, anxieties, apathy, depression, and hostility. In *The Bach Flower Remedies*, he sets forth his insights into health and illness—plus a remarkable system for treating the "ills of heart and spirit" with flower remedies.

The Bach Flower Remedies is actually three books in one. In the first section, "Heal Thyself," Dr. Bach discusses his spiritual perspective on the nature of illness and the ultimate source of effective cures to illness—the divinity within us. In specific, Dr. Bach says the human weaknesses that lead to illness need to be washed away by flooding our consciousness with a strong dose of the spiritual qualities that will neutralize them. To aid in this process, Dr. Bach recommends the use of flower remedies—the essences of flowers which, when taken in the form of elixirs, act as antidotes to the emotional poisons which lead to illness.

The use of these remedies is described in the book's second section, "The Twelve Healers." The final section, "The Bach Remedies Repertory" by F.J. Wheeler, M.D., is a detailed account of the value of each of the 38 flower remedies and how to use them.

Just reading this book is a health-giving experience. But its real power lies in using the remedies to bring us back into harmony with the God within us—and the divine power of Love.

War in Heaven
by Charles Williams

The place is England; the time is the 1930's. A number of different factions—an Anglican priest, a Catholic duke, the bewildered employees of a publishing house, a nasty crowd of satanists, and a powerful mage who is the magical "protector" of the graal—are vying with one another in search of the holy graal, the cup which Jesus used at the Last Supper.

The graal means something quite different to each group. It is a doorway to power for the satanists, a historical oddity to the publishers, an immensely significant relic to the duke, a point where the love of God can be experienced to the priest, and a visible symbol of the presence of God on earth to its protector.

Against a thrilling plot of supernatural mystery and murder, Williams weaves a masterful theme: that the real graal is the soul—the true vessel of spirit within us—and the ultimate prize of our spiritual search is its power, love, and wisdom. In the novel, the graal is first stolen, then attacked psychically, and finally almost destroyed. Simultaneously, the lives and sanity of many of the major characters undergo similar assaults and perils. In the end, however, divine powers triumph and evil is defeated through the courageous acts of a few of the characters.

The real war in heaven is the struggle within us among the elements of our personal weakness and our spiritual strength. Charles Williams has written a powerful novel which does justice to this important theme. It should be read by all students of the mysteries of the spiritual path.

Clairvoyant Investigations
by Geoffrey Hodson

Geoffrey Hodson was one of the truly great clairvoyants of the twentieth century. This new book was one of his final projects—and it is a fitting culmination to a distinguished career.

Hodson picks two of his favorite themes for further clairvoyant investigation—the angelic kingdom and the power of music. After a brief introduction to both subjects, he goes on to describe in great detail his clairvoyant observations and their significance. In many cases, these observations are complemented by stunning color illustrations of what Hodson saw psychically.

In the section on angels, Hodson carefully documents the interaction of angels of various grades with the forces of nature, with the vital energy of the earth, with solar energy, and with the healing of humanity. But he does not just describe what he "sees," as fascinating as this is—he also describes the inner depths of consciousness in these angelic powers. As such, there is much we can learn about our own consciousness.

In the section on music, Hodson examines the forces and forms set in motion by the performance of music by humans, the angelic beings this attracts, and the impact of music on our own consciousness. Perhaps the most fascinating observations are those dealing with the effect of holy music, although the pieces he examines range from "Greensleeves" to Bach.

Clairvoyant Investigations is a beautifully illustrated book with a powerful presence of its own.

Myth Conceptions
by Robert Asprin

A demon who has lost his powers, Aahz still manages to keep his apprentice, Skeeve, out of most kinds of trouble. Then Skeeve is summoned to audition for the post of Court Magician. Unfortunately, he gets the job.

How can Aahz and Skeeve defend the kingdom against the mightiest army in the world? If they win, they will be executed—and if they lose, they will be killed. What kind of magic can beat these odds?

A very rare kind of magic, indeed—the magic of author Robert Asprin, who has combined a rollicking good sense of humor with high fantasy to shape a story in *Myth Conceptions* that reminds us that life is filled with things that are not what they seem to be. We need the good sense to laugh at life and see it for what it really is.

Myth Conceptions is packed with fast paced adventures revolving around Aahz, Skeeve, a king who tries not to reign, and an army which is actually fighting only so it can pay off its bar and gambling bills.

In each case, the public image or myth of each character differs vastly from his or her private nature. At times, this embarrasses them—but other times the myth saves them from disaster, as it affects the way everyone else treats them.

Myth Conceptions reminds us that there are often contradictions between what we seem to be and who we actually are. Sometimes we stumble over the myth; sometimes we live up to it; but in either case, our personal myth helps us stretch our character.

This is a book no one should myth.

The New View
Over Atlantis
by John Michell

In 1921, the British merchant Alfred Watkins had a psychic vision which propelled him centuries into the past and revealed to him a precise network of straight lines crisscrossing the English countryside in a geometric pattern. Watkins realized that churches, monuments, roads, and earthworks had all been built on these lines, as though there were a purpose linking them all in some mysterious way. He came to call these channels "ley lines."

Watkin's announcement of ley lines led to a renewed interest in the significance of geomantic design. Eight years later, for example, Kathryn Maltwood found that the landscape about Glastonbury Cathedral was filled with mounds and natural folds representing the signs of the zodiac. Other keen observers made similar discoveries as well, finding that the ancient Druids had used hills, springs, plains, and rivers to form temples several miles in length.

But brilliant and important discoveries often fade into the background after an initial flurry of interest— and this seemed to be the fate of these discoveries until the publication in 1969 of *The View Over Atlantis* by John Michell. Michell had researched the work of Watkins, Maltwood, and others, updated it, and retold it in an absorbing and stimulating book.

Now, Michell has updated his own work and issued *The **New** View Over Atlantis*, with a great deal of additional material. Like the earlier book, this one gives a full account of ley lines, and then goes on to present a new commentary on the mystical signifi-cance of numbers in ancient architecture and city planning.

Underlying it all is the very strong thesis that the ley lines are to the earth what acupuncture meridians are to the etheric body of the human being. Michell pre-sents striking evidence that the planet earth is not just an inert ball of dirt and rock, but actually *a living body of giant intelligence with arteries of living energy that circulates throughout the surface of the earth.* The ancients, he suggests, knew of this living nature of physical energy and took it into account as they planned their cities, temples, and landscaping.

One of the most fascinating aspects of this book is the deft way in which Michell documents knowledge of ley lines in all cultures throughout the world. In one chapter, for instance, he delves into Chinese myths and geomancy. According to Michell, there is a strong tradition in China for facilitating the unimpeded flow of the earth's vital energy by moving hills and redirect-ing streams. The Chinese are also careful to locate shrines, burial sites, and homes in conjunction with these lines.

Michell also brilliantly relates the mythological sym-bolism of the dragon in China with similar myths in English folklore. The Chinese dragon is actually an aspect of the earth's vitality. It flows along the ley lines, bringing an extra charge of energy to the land. In early English myths, the dragon is much the same—a great benevolent power that is a source of natural vitality when properly tamed and focused. The idea that the dragon is an evil force apparently arose only after the Church became threatened by these pagan tales and sought ways to discredit them.

The second half of the book, in which Michell discusses the mystical value of numbers, is equally fascinating. Ancient sacred buildings, he found, were built not only at the crossing of two or more ley lines, but also in accord with mystical symbolism and the structure of numbers. Number was held by the ancients to be the first archetype of nature, with everything in creation eventually conforming to this order in terms of its shapes, patterns, and cycles.

This is a remarkable book, not just for the information it imparts but also for the way it stimulates the thinking mind. Colin Wilson, the author of *The Mind Parasites*, hailed *The New View Over Atlantis* as "one of the great seminal books of our generation."

Michell himself makes the point that "revelation comes to those who invoke it through intense studies and a lively curiosity of mind." *The New View Over Atlantis* stands as a lucid revelation of the relationship between myth and civilization, alchemy and science, and astronomy and acupuncture.

As Michell writes, "No form of study can be more delightful and beneficial than this one, for in pondering the designs and works of the ancient sages one is exposed to the noblest mentalities of our kind, which these works reflect." For this reason alone, *The New View Over Atlantis* is a book to be read by every thinking person.

Glory Road
by Robert Heinlein

"There are things which cannot be taught in ten easy lessons, nor popularized for the masses; they take years of sweat. This be treason in an age when ignorance has come into its own and one man's opinion is as good as another's. But there it is."

Treason, of course, is just a tiny "t" beyond "reason." And, in the marvelous fantasy world of Robert Heinlein, treason to three-car garages, cocktail parties, and similar cultural "necessities" leads us out of the kingdom of ignorance and onto the glory road.

The glory road, in this particular case, begins on a beach of the French Riviera and ends at the center of the cosmos. Scar, a young American, is asked by Star, the empress of 20 universes, to help her retrieve the Egg of the Phoenix, which contains the knowledge of all her predecessors, from the dreaded Soul-Eater, who stole it from her.

Before the egg is regained, it becomes clear that the betrayal of ignorance and materialism is anything *but* treason. It is the stuff of which true heroes—and the spiritual life—are made. For the glory road is really the spiritual path. To travel it, one must be ready to leave behind the roads the average person chooses to follow. He must embrace the magic of the soul and marry himself to its strength. And he must defeat the obstacles which would knock him off the path.

As such, *Glory Road* is as much an adventure into our *own* assumptions, beliefs, and heroism as it is a story of Scar and Star. For anyone who likes fantasy, this is a glorious novel.

Health & Light
by John N. Ott

John Ott had a serious health problem. Arthritis in his hip had become so severe that he was constantly in pain and had to use a cane to walk. Medication failed to produce any improvement; the only remaining hope was surgery. Then Ott accidentally broke his glasses. One day shortly thereafter, he decided to do some outside work, limping about as best he could— even though his new glasses had not yet arrived. After an hour, he suddenly felt better—and did not need the cane. He began walking up and down the driveway and discovered he was free of the pain which had crippled him so long. Then he *ran* into his house and up the stairs to tell his wife what had happened.

An ordinary individual would have dismissed this as nothing but an odd set of coincidences. But Ott had been studying the relationship between light and health for a number of years. As the developer of time lapse photography, he had often noted that many plants do not grow well indoors under artificial lighting. He had even conducted experiments which led him to suspect that not all kinds of light are equal. Sunlight, he had found, is far superior to artificial lighting. Ott therefore began to suspect that his glasses had been keeping certain portions of sunlight, most notably the ultraviolet rays, from entering his eyes. When he broke them and could wear them no longer, and then went outside, the ultraviolet once again was able to enter his system. And that, he surmised, somehow had a beneficial influence on his arthritis.

44

His curiosity piqued, Ott began a series of experiments into the need of the human system for a full spectrum of light. *Health and Light* is his report of what he has discovered. Quite briefly, Ott has found that many of us suffer from light malnutrition—and are affected both physically and emotionally by these deficiences. He has discovered, for example, that:

• Tinted glasses and sunglasses can increase emotional reactiveness and vulnerability to illness.

• Television radiation can induce hyperkinesis and fatigue.

• The proper use of light can help treat cancer.

• Flourescent lighting can increase headaches and insomnia.

• Ultraviolet light, transmitted through the pineal and pituitary glands, is important to the regulation of the endocrine system.

The story of these discoveries—and Ott's recommendations for improving our "diet" of light—is one of the true scientific breakthroughs of the last quarter century. It is the story of an observant, intelligent man who acted upon his observations and then supported them with scientific experimentation.

The importance of light has long been known esoterically. But it has largely been ignored by science. This book is the first step toward correcting this deficiency. It will lead the intelligent investigator to realize that light affects all of our vehicles—the mental, emotional, and etheric bodies, as well as the physical form—and can enter the human system through either the physical body or any of these subtle bodies.

The only vehicle which is responsive to light in just one location (the eyes) is the dense physical body.

Each of the more subtle bodies can absorb the subtle radiations of sunlight at any spot on its surface. This can be very useful in healing, since the subtle is always capable of energizing the gross. Treating the mental body with light will also help the astral, the etheric, and the dense physical forms.

It is important to see Ott's remarkable work in this larger context. Ott's research has verified the basic esoteric fact that we are multidimensional beings, and has shown that light influences us not just physically, but emotionally and mentally as well.

It also provides a fascinating insight into the standard operating procedures of scientific circles. Having discovered some obviously important principles, Ott has largely met with stony indifference and outright attack from scientific authorities.

Health and Light is an important book. Its anecdotal style makes it easy and absorbing reading; its scientific content makes its statements on light authoritative. It is a book everyone should read.

The Destiny of America
by Robert R. Leichtman, M.D.

"This country was divinely inspired," observes the spirit of Theodore Roosevelt. "It was created through divine intervention—through the acts of people in tune with divine will."

But modern America has lost much of its divine vision and is veering off course. This is the strong but timely message of Roosevelt and six other leaders from America's past—Alexander Hamilton, Thomas Jefferson, Benjamin Franklin, Franklin Delano Roosevelt, Harry Truman, and George Washington.

They deliver this message in a powerful new book, *The Destiny of America*, the final book in the 24-volume series *From Heaven to Earth*. It is the report of a conversation conducted mediumistically by Dr. Robert R. Leichtman with these spirits.

Beginning with Hamilton and ending with a stirring summation by Washington, the leaders raise the flag to warn us that we have given away much of the freedom they fought to establish and preserve. In particular, we have lost the economic freedom which made America great, have compromised our democracy by allowing a huge bureaucracy to develop, and have lost sight of the ideals we are meant to demonstrate as a world leader.

The interview is filled with brilliant insights into the ideals and principles of the spirit of America—and suggestions for what we can do to restore our freedoms.

The Destiny of America is probably the most important book published this year.

The Earthsea Trilogy
by Ursula LeGuin

One of the classic themes of literature is the eternal conflict between good and evil, and its role in the creative process. Seldom has this theme been treated as effectively as it is in Ursula LeGuin's trilogy of novels: *The Wizard of Earthsea*, *The Tombs of Atuan*, and *The Farthest Shore*.

This exciting and fast-paced set of novels records the Odyssey of Ged, one of the greatest archmages or wizards in the history of Earthsea, a group of islands on a world not unlike our own.

As *The Wizard of Earthsea* begins, Ged is only a boy, known to most as "Sparrowhawk." He soon finds he has a natural instinct for magic. At first, he uses his power only to amuse himself, but after he uses his gift to save his village from an invasion, he undergoes rigorous training.

In the midst of this training, however, his youthful pride overwhelms him, and he foolishly unleashes a dark, malevolent power, almost killing himself. From that point on, the dark force he has unloosed begins to stalk Ged.

Ged's struggle to defeat this shadow which pursues him is symbolic of the many difficulties we all face as we travel our path—our Odyssey—and confront our weaknesses. At first, Ged believes the evil to be outside himself, an ancient power which reentered the world during his moment of magical folly. He sees himself as the hunted, and despairs of escape.

Slowly, though, his attitude changes, and Ged becomes the hunter, not the hunted. He chases the dark force about the world, finally engaging it in a battle to the death at the edge of the earth. Only then, in this extreme state, does Ged realize he cannot escape it, for it is *within*. He is dealing with his own dark nature. This recognition enables him to triumph.

In *The Tombs of Atuan*, the narrative shifts to the training of Arha, the priestess of the Tombs, the Domain of the Nameless Ones, the gods of an ancient religion. As priestess, Arha must guard the Tombs and their large underground labyrinth, which is the repository of much power and ancient treasures.

The life of Arha is quiet and undisturbed, until Ged arrives as a thief in the night, to search the tombs for a ring which long ago was the property of Erreth-Akbe, the most powerful magician Earthsea had ever known. When almost defeated by evil, Erreth-Akbe broke the ring and hid the two parts. Ever since, Earthsea has not been at peace.

Having found one half of the ring, Ged is searching for the other half. Arha discovers Ged and decides to destroy him, but finds herself strangely reluctant to do so. Eventually, Ged convinces Arha that she guards the powers of darkness, not the powers of light.

Ged finds the second half of the ring and unites the two, but he is still controlled by Arha, just as the far more powerful and wise force of our spirit often becomes trapped by the doubting, materialistic grip of the earthbound personality dominated by superstition, tradition, fear, and ritual.

Working only with his wisdom, love, and faith, Ged does eventually conquer Arha's mind and will, leading her to forsake her underground labyrinths and religious dogma and embrace her true individuality.

In the third novel, *The Farthest Shore*, Ged has become the archmage of Earthsea, the most powerful of all wizards. As such, he must confront a problem afflicting the whole of civilization: the magical power of Earthsea is quickly fading. Since magic is essential to almost everything in Earthsea, even manufacture, the failure of magic is a dire threat.

After many adventures, Ged discovers that the cause of this problem is a selfish magician who has sought to attain physical immortality by sucking the life out of everything around him. To confront him, Ged travels first to the farthest shore of Earthsea, and then to an even farther shore, passing into the land of the dead. With the help of dragons, Ged destroys his opponent and closes the door between the forces of darkness and light, before returning to his own body.

Through this story of battle between one who serves the divine plan and one who is selfish at the expense of everyone else, we are given a rich and symbolic description of the conflicts which plague our own civilization.

Indeed, these three stories are much, much more than just enchanting tales. They translate the everyday struggles of the spiritual aspirant to mythical proportions, giving us a framework in which to view our own problems more intelligently. They also help us see the power of the magic in our lives—the magic of spirit.

The Earthsea Trilogy is a work of magic itself.

The Secret Teachings of All Ages
by Manly P. Hall

Manly P. Hall is one of this century's most important chroniclers of the mysteries of the spiritual life, and *The Secret Teachings of All Ages* is unquestionably the keystone of his writings, a rich and marvelous treasure of esoteric knowledge.

Amply illustrated and handsomely printed, *The Secret Teachings of All Ages* is a compendium of occult lore—and a delight to read. There is an incredible wealth of information in this volume, covering every major area of the mysteries:

- Atlantis.
- The Egyptian & Greek mysteries.
- Astrology.
- The Qabalah.
- The Tarot.
- Alchemy.
- The science of numbers.
- The esoteric roots of freemasonry.
- The esoteric message of the major world religions.

This is not a book that espouses a limited doctrine; it is broad and expansive, embracing all of the major esoteric and spiritual traditions of the world and demonstrating the contributions each has made to world thought and understanding. As such, it is a book which can help acquaint us with the tremendous depth of human knowledge.

The Secret Teachings of All Ages is an encyclopedic book that belongs in the library of everyone seriously interested in the mysteries of life.

Across the Unknown
by Stewart Edward White

Before he began writing books based on the psychic explorations of his wife Betty, Stewart Edward White was already a well-established writer of adventure stories—stories of the wild west, untamed Africa, and frigid Alaska. So it was only natural for White to consider the psychic investigations of his wife one more kind of adventure in uncharted regions.

Indeed, *Across the Unknown,* is much more than testimony that such dimensions do exist. It is a comprehensive effort to map these inner regions of consciousness and *make the unknown known.* But White is not satisfied with giving us only a vicarious tour of the invisible levels of life. He insists on showing us how to make the journey *on our own,* so that we are not dependent on anyone else's testimony.

The result is an esoteric masterpiece—a practical, easy-to-read, and entertaining description of what it truly means to refine our awareness and nurture the ability to operate consciously at all levels of our being, the intuitive as well as the physical.

As White puts it, *Across the Unknown* is "a formula for living." It reveals how the inner dimensions are alive in each of us, even while immersed in the physical plane. And it shows us how to tap the reality of the unknown to enrich our life.

Across the Unknown is one of the most important books ever written about the inner planes. As Betty says, "It is essential to linger frequently on the frontier of one's limitations, looking out eagerly *across the unknown.*" This book helps us do just that.

Initiation
by Elisabeth Haich

"The higher self—God—always finds a human mouth when he has a message for us. For the *self* there is no such thing as an obstacle."

There is no such thing as an obstacle. This quiet phrase, ending a chapter near the conclusion of this epic novel, nicely sums up the spirit that pervades the whole of the book. Because *Initiation* is a story of great internal struggle and conflict—and a story of failure to seize the opportunity of initiation. And yet, even failure of this magnitude becomes not disgrace, but the basis for triumph. In this dramatic way, we vividly learn that there truly is no obstacle which can defeat the soul.

This is an autobiographical novel, set both at the time of the second world war and in ancient Egypt. It is the story of a twentieth-century aspirant who does not fully understand the powerful struggle of her life, until she psychically remembers her training for initiation in the mystery temples of Egypt, the trials of the initiation itself, and the unredeemed weakness which leads her to fail the test.

But she does not really fail. The test merely continues on and is resumed, after a series of lives, in this century, against the backdrop of war. In this way, we are subtly reminded that the tests of the individual transpire in the context of the tests of humanity. The initiation of the individual makes sense only in the context of the initiation of humanity.

There is a great measure of wisdom in *Initiation*. It, too, has a message from the higher self to us.

The Fountainhead
by Ayn Rand

Ayn Rand writes novels which are set in "the way things are," but move us toward a deeper, more profound realization of "the way things ought to be."

In *The Fountainhead*, Miss Rand tells the story of Howard Roark, an architect who refuses to surrender either his individuality or his creative integrity. He thereby incurs the wrath and opposition of most of the rest of the characters—petty people who neither appreciate nor understand Roark's genius. They are attracted to Roark by the thought of benefiting from his talent. But when they find they cannot profit from it, they turn against him and seek to destroy him.

To Ayn Rand, Howard Roark sums up the ideals of self-actualization and creative genius. He is a man who has tapped the "fountainhead" of inspiration and brilliance within himself, and is guided by it, in spite of the bitter opposition he encounters. He is a man about whom Miss Rand can write, quoting Nietzsche, "The noble soul has reverence for itself."

It is rare to find an author who recognizes the inherent nobility of human life and presents it in its proper light, not romanticizing it but forcefully dramatizing its strength, its value, its purpose, and its reality. It is likewise rare to find a novel which so continually prods us to *think* and reevaluate our idea of what counts in life.

The Fountainhead is a classic of modern American literature. It deserves to be—and it deserves to be read by everyone striving to fulfill the promise of human nobility and genius.

The Hour Glass
by Carl Japikse

The fable has long been a favorite device for convey-ing esoteric truths as well as entertaining and delight-ing readers. *The Hour Glass* is a collection of fables spun in the inventive mind of Carl Japikse.

But these are fables with a *difference*, for each one contains a grain of sand which, as it trickles through the hour glass of an inquiring mind, magically trans-forms itself into a growing seed of new understand-ing—about time, conflict, wisdom, creativity, ingen-uity, pride, courage, and the most fundamental themes of human living. They are fables that will charm children, but *enlighten* adults.

This delightful set of stories embraces a wide range of fabulous characters—from an artistic donkey and an intellectual coyote to a politicking baboon and a messianic minnow. There are even a few fables about men and women—60 fables in all, one for each minute the sands of the hour glass mark as they tumble on their journey through time.

Many of the fables are written so that they may be used as a focus for our contemplative thinking or meditation. As such, they are really parables reveal-ing something of divine life, as well as fables com-menting on the foibles and foolishness of human life. As might be expected, one of Japikse's favorite themes is the esoteric potential of time.

The fables are accompanied by 21 drawings by Mark Peyton which are just as delightful as the stories. *The Hour Glass* is a refreshing, original collection.

The Mind Parasites

by Colin Wilson

Surely one of the most important pieces of fiction to emerge so far in this century is *The Mind Parasites*, a novel by Colin Wilson. First published in 1967, it is a powerful story about the reactiveness found in the collective subconscious of humanity, how it influences the average person, and how it can be overcome.

In brief, *The Mind Parasites* is a science fiction tale about the archeologist Gilbert Austin and his confrontation with the Tsathogguans, denizens of the mental deep who in effect attempt to take control of human civilization. They endeavor to destroy Austin and his colleagues, but as Austin discovers their true nature, he grows in his understanding and capacity to destroy them.

Ultimately, the action leads to global warfare, the psychokinetic movement of the moon, and final victory in outer space. Yet for all these exciting and suspenseful adventures, the real story of *The Mind Parasites* transpires at a deeper, more profound dimension—in the collective subconscious of the human race.

There *is* a collective subconscious for the whole race, and it is just as real and active as our own personal subconsciouses. It is filled with the collective fears, animosities, laziness, and parasitism of the human race—and has been building in force and scope since the beginning of mankind.

In no way is this collective subconscious to be confused with the noble and divine spirit which all humanity share; that would more appropriately be called the "supraconscious." The collective subconscious, by contrast, is entirely of mankind's own making. While some of the elements within it are good and partly enlightened, many of them are not. The collective subconscious has very strong attitudes about what is right and proper and works hard to preserve the status quo. It enshrines pettiness, the lowest common denominator, and mob attitudes, such as violence.

One of the repeated themes in *The Mind Parasites* is that this collective subconscious will fight any radical departure from the norms of society, including genius. Indeed, the novel begins with the suicide of a close friend of Austin's—a man of brilliance who learned too much about the nature of the mind parasites and thus became a threat. In retaliation, the parasites drove him to suicide.

To some who read this book, it may seem to be a novel of paranoia, but it most assuredly is not. It is a brilliant description of the psychic reality of the collective subconscious and its persistent resistance to new ideas, genius, and individuality. Time and again, it drives home the message that mass consciousness will attack and even try to destroy men and women of genius. It is sad but true that people of genius appear and thrive *in spite of* mass consciousness.

In many ways, *The Mind Parasites* is virtually a textbook on how to neutralize the influence of mass consciousness. As Austin meets challenge after challenge, he discovers the absolute necessity of focusing the personal will to overcome his own self-doubt and the intrusion of alien ideas into his thinking.

But even that, he finds, is limited in its value. He

learns that this personal will must be used in a larger perspective, not as an expression of one's selfishness. And the power of the personal will is not just something to *believe* in; it must be dynamically expressed as well.

Ultimately, he learns that it is the overshadowing power of divine love, blended with the will, which is most effective in meeting the resistance of the mind parasites. From that point on, Austin is clearly in charge of the situation; we do not doubt that he will triumph, but there are still a number of surprises involved in just how he manages to do it.

This is a novel of tremendous insight—a story which totally captivates the imagination of the perceptive reader. Once begun, it is nearly impossible to set down; once finished, it is put away reluctantly, with the wish that it were longer. This wish is mitigated, however, by the realization that here is a book worth rereading several times.

There is a River
by Thomas Sugrue

It has now been more than forty years since the death of Edgar Cayce. At that time, his work as a psychic was little known. Now, thanks to a number of popular biographies and countless books on his readings, Edgar Cayce has become the best-known psychic in America. When people first start reading about the inner life and spiritual growth, it is almost surely a book about Cayce that they begin with.

Yet with all the profusion of books about Cayce and his work, the very first one ever written, Thomas Sugrue's *There is a River*, remains by far the best biography and introduction to Cayce's philosophy and readings. In all likelihood, this is because it is written by a professional author who knew Cayce as a friend, and was therefore able to draw on first-hand research, not just the myths and interpretations which have arisen over the years since Cayce died.

And the story of *There is a River* is a fascinating one. Cayce richly deserves the fame which has come to him; during his life, he gave more than 15,000 trance readings in which he diagnosed physical problems and suggested cures, reported on previous lives and karmic residue, advised on spiritual growth, and even gave suggestions for business and creative projects. He also had the foresight to have these trances stenographically recorded, so the transcripts would be available for further research. It is this treasure which he left behind which makes his work so valuable.

There is a River is a marvelous introduction to the life and work of an important psychic.

Healing & Regeneration Through Color & Music

by Corinne Heline

The many colors of light, as well as the many tones of music, are different wavelengths of living energy. We are affected by the colors and music of our environment and—if we understand the esoteric principles of energy—we can harness both color and music to heal ourselves and others, mentally, emotionally, and physically.

Corinne Heline studied the impact of the energies of color and music throughout her long career in new age work, and wrote two classics on the subject, *Healing and Regeneration Through Color* and *Healing and Regeneration Through Music.* These two books have now been combined in a single volume, *Healing and Regeneration Through Color and Music.*

In her essay on color, Mrs. Heline explores the esoteric principles of color, its supernatural powers, its relationship to music, and how it can be used both for healing physical ailments and building solid character values. In the treatise on music, she expands on the same themes, but applies them to the principle of harmony and musical tones. She also explores some of the deeper significances of great music.

These two essays are especially powerful because of the many practical suggestions Mrs. Heline makes for the use of both color and music. She packs a tremendous amount of information into a relatively short space—information that each reader will be able to readily use for healing and regeneration.

This is a first-rate source of insight.

OM
The Secret of Ahbor Valley
by Talbot Mundy

Back in the days of British rule in India, an unusual piece of jade happens to come into the hands of the head of the British secret service. Wanting to discover its origin, he assigns Cottswold Ommony, one of his agents, to find out the story of this mysterious jewel.

The pursuit of this jewel leads Ommony on perhaps the greatest mystery of all—the journey into the inner levels of human awareness. For this fist-sized piece of jade has an unusual power to stimulate the mind of the one who gazes into it. In those who are selfish and corrupt, it will reveal the flaws of the dark side of their nature. But in those who are in tune with spirit, it will quicken the higher levels of consciousness.

Ommony's effort to trace the origin of the jade leads him to suspect the motives and acts of a Tibetan lama named Tsiang Samdup. He becomes convinced that Samdup is involved in all manner of nefarious crimes, not the least of which is purchasing young orphaned white girls and transporting them to Ahbor Valley—which is said to be the home of the Masters, but is also known to be a place of great danger. It is said that the natives kill all strangers who enter the district.

Ommony, in fact, has a personal link with Ahbor Valley, because his sister and her husband disappeared there twenty years earlier.

Samdup tours India with a group of actors, presenting metaphysical plays in one small village after another. Ommony suspects that the theatrical group is a front for what he believes to be Samdup's criminal

activities, so he disguises himself as a native Indian actor and joins the cast. He is able to pull off the deception quite successfully, because he is fluent in several Indian languages, although apparently he does not actually fool Samdup.

By being a part of the cast, Ommony also becomes acquainted with Samding, a young protege of Samdup who plays the role of a venerated Indian saint. The play is about kings and peasants who trade places, believing that it is their roles in life which make them what they are, not their character. But as the play reveals, a good person is good no matter what his place in society, just as a greedy, dishonest person remains selfish no matter what his station.

The theme of the play is not always well received, however, as it is a direct attack on the traditional Indian caste system. Performances often lead to riots, and the group is usually forced to leave the village immediately after the play ends.

Suddenly, Samdup leaves the group and departs for an unknown destination. Ommony finds out that Samding is not really a young man, as he had thought, but in fact his own niece, the daughter of his sister and brother-in-law! She was born shortly before her parents died and was saved from death herself by Samdup. More astounding, Samding is in fact the reincarnation of the great saint she has been portraying in the play! Samdup is her teacher.

Ommony could give over his quest at this point, but decides to press on. He traces Samdup into Ahbor Valley, risking both his own life and that of Samdup, who must protect him. The true relationship of Samdup as teacher and Ommony as pupil—soul and personality—comes out into the open, and Samdup instructs Ommony in the ways of the inner life.

Om, The Secret of Ahbor Valley is truly a masterpiece of esoteric fiction and one of Talbot Mundy's greatest novels. It deftly illustrates the true way in which the soul guides and instructs the personality, always leading it but never commanding it. The free will choice of Ommony to pursue the jade and then Samdup is always his own. He is never forced to continue the journey.

The trials and tribulations Ommony encounters—as well as the false suspicions he harbors about Samdup—are likewise powerfully symbolic of the tests and hardships of the spiritual path. Mundy writes with a clear understanding of what the life of spirit requires, yet spins his story into an enjoyable, high-spirited, and exciting tale of adventure.

At the end, Samdup shows Ommony the original piece of jade from which the smaller chip was taken— a jewel of such spiritual power that it is studied only by the most advanced spiritual students. And Ommony learns that his niece is to serve as an avatar for modern India, bringing a new message of spirit—a message which surely will be as revolutionary and controversial as the one Jesus brought the Palestinians in His day. Ommony, too, has a role he can play, if he so chooses—to serve as his niece's guide and to assist her in bringing this message to India.

It is on this note—a note of excitement, revelation, and triumph—that *Om, The Secret of Ahbor Valley*, concludes. It is truly a novel which can lead the reader as well as the hero to a new awareness of the treasure within. It is itself a treasure not to pass by.

A Soul's Journey
by Peter Richelieu

Out-of-body travel has long been a fascinating topic for occult writers, but most books on the subject have been nothing more than travelogues exploring the author's own rich fantasies. Peter Richelieu's *A Soul's Journey*, however, offers a great deal more than the standard fare. It is a first-hand account of travel in the various levels of the astral and mental planes.

The book is written in narrative style, recounting the journeys of Henry, an Englishman living in Ceylon at the time of the second world war. The account begins with Henry grieving over the death of his brother Charles, a British solider. His grief invokes the appearance of Acharya, a holy man from India, who lectures him about the phenomena of the inner life and events after death.

But Acharya's instruction does not stop there. Using special techniques, he enables Henry to leave his body during the hours of sleep so that he can be taken on a guided tour of the inner, subtle planes of creation. Each night, Henry takes a powerful drug to ensure sleep and travels in his subtle bodies through many adventures on the subplanes of the astral and mental levels.

First, Acharya leads Henry to visit his brother Charles, to see that he has not actually "died." After that, Henry is taught much about the rich opportunities of the inner planes for education and growth—both for the so-called "dead" and for people who can visit the inner planes while asleep.

It is rare to find a book which gives any description

of the inner planes except those levels closest to the physical. It should be understood that this book is not just an account of the pretty scenery we might encounter at low psychic levels. Instead, Richelieu provides us with a clear account of the hospitals and colleges of the inner planes, the great halls of knowledge and wisdom. In addition, there are interesting reports of how spirits visit the physical plane and mingle among us, usually without our awareness.

Henry learns about the training given to people when they first arrive on the inner planes after death and observes several occult and religious ceremonies first-hand. Eventually, he is taken by Acharya to the mental plane. It is likely that this is the only book in print, outside the writings of C.W. Leadbeater, which gives an accurate account of the uncanny experiences of dealing directly with the force of ideas, communicating telepathically, and being totally free of cloying emotions.

The use of a drug to visit the inner planes may be a bit of fiction, as it would not be a standard spiritual practice. But this is *not* a book on how to leave the body and travel on the inner planes. It is a rare and unusually precise account of the nature and activities of the inner life.

Far from describing the heaven worlds as places of "rest" and "peace," which is silly, *A Soul's Journey* leads us into a realm of tremendous activity, healing, and teaching. The book emphasizes the fact that we all have a rich life on the inner planes, whether or not we can visit them consciously, as a result of having finer bodies made of the subtle matter of these inner realms. Thus, it is possible to be taught and healed on these inner levels, even while still in the physical body. Richelieu opens to us many new possibilities for extending the range of our education and experience— while our physical body sleeps.

One of the most important messages for all of us to learn is that we have an existence on the inner side of life *right now*, not just after we die. We are all endowed with the potential to tap the higher dimensions of life, even while in the physical.

Reading *A Soul's Journey* helps give us fresh insight into this dynamic principle. Even though most of us are not likely to have vivid conscious memories of what transpires on the inner planes while we are asleep, as Henry did, we do tend to bring through the wisdom we gain into our waking hours, as nudges, insights, and new awareness. It is valuable to learn as much about this process as possible. Richelieu also leaves us with much to ponder on regarding the influences of the higher dimensions on our activities here in the physical plane.

In fact, *A Soul's Journey* is really everyone's odyssey.

(*Originally published as* **From The Turret**)

Prodigal Genius
by John J. O'Neill

Nikola Tesla spent his lifetime making the impossible possible—and doing it with brilliance, style, and seeming ease. He made practical the generation of alternating current, which electrical scientists had thought impossible. He developed a system for long distance transmission of electricity, which Thomas Edison had thought impossible. He broadcast electricity through the air without wires, which many experts *still* think impossible. He was truly a prodigal genius.

Prodigal Genius is the story of Nikola Tesla's life and work. It is not just a biography of Tesla, however. It is also one of the most remarkable explorations of human genius and creativity in print. For within the story of Tesla's life there is another story as well—the story of an enlightened and noble mind at work, examining the archetypal laws and patterns of the universe and *doing something with them!*

There are important lessons in this book for every reader—lessons about creativity, the enlightened use of energy, the psychic aspects of genius, and the tendency of the public to ignore its greatest geniuses. Some of the lessons are subtle and lie between the lines, but the story is so skillfully told that we are inspired to look for them—and learn.

While many biographies have now been written about Tesla, John O'Neill's still stands as the most insightful. O'Neill knew Tesla personally, and was a Pulitzer Prize-winning author of scientific writings.

Like Tesla himself, this biography *glows*.

The Dragonriders of Pern
by Anne McCaffrey

Every few hundred years, mysterious threads drop on Pern from outer space. If allowed to fall to the ground, they would quickly destroy all vegetation, and Pern would be devastated. There is only one way to fight the threads: the dragons of Pern, guided by their skillful riders, are able to burn the strands before they touch the ground, by belching fire at them.

The skill required to ride the dragons is great, and it separates the riders from the rest of the people of Pern. The riders develop an intense bond with their dragons, and are able to communicate telepathically with them. Eventually, they learn to travel through time as well.

Still, the skills of the dragonriders are not always appreciated—especially since the interval between the threats of the threads is so long. The society of Pern becomes divided between those who champion the dragonriders and those who scorn them.

In *The Dragonriders of Pern*, Anne McCaffrey has created a fascinating world, Pern, in which exciting and deeply symbolic adventures unfold. It is hard to read these three novels—*Dragonflight*, *Dragonfire*, and *The White Dragon*—without soon seeing the parallels between the dragons and our own subconscious, and between the threads and the thought patterns of mass consciousness which would seek to control us.

There is much fire and drama in these three novels—and plenty of adventure.

Music:
Its Secret Influence Throughout the Ages
by Cyril Scott

Music is a language that speaks directly to the subconscious. If of high quality, it can carry us into the inner realms of spirit. Such is the impact of good classical music, which inspires us with sympathy, courage, and adoration for God. If of low quality, it can damage the emotions, provoking selfishness, sensuality, and even violence—the impact of jazz and rock and roll.

Cyril Scott's remarkable book, *Music: Its Secret Influence Throughout the Ages*, explores the psychic impact of music and reveals its potential for healing or harming the quality of life. The author was an eminent British composer and esotericist. His observations are an important contribution to psychic literature.

He states, for example, that much damage is being done to society through the widespread playing of various forms of popular music. Much of this effect is subliminal and beyond our conscious recognition—but is destructive nonetheless.

Classical music, on the other hand, can have an uplifting effect. The author explains that much classical music is inspired by angels, who work with trained musicians with the capacity to be impressed intuitively by divine themes. He explores the impact this form of inspiration had on such great composers as Beethoven, Chopin, Bach, Handel, Wagner, and others.

This is an important book for anyone interested in music or the psychic life.

The Magic of Xanth
by Piers Anthony

Xanth is a magical kingdom, not at all like Mundania, where there is no magic. In Xanth, everything is either magical or a creation of magic. Trees cast spells to prevent people from cutting them down. Animals talk. There are centaurs, dragons, and gnomes. And every human being has a special magical talent. If he does not, then he is exiled to Mundania.

The stories of Xanth begin with *A Spell for Chameleon*. A young man, Bink, has been unable to demonstrate any magical skill, even though the charts insist he does have magic. And so he is forced into exile, where he meets Chameleon, a woman who is trying to escape from her magical talents, and Trent, the evil ex-king of Xanth. He also discovers his unique magical talent—a talent so great that he is able to help Chameleon accept herself and Trent become a redeemed man, once again king of Xanth.

The remaining two novels in this set—*The Source of Magic* and *Castle Roogna*—continue in much the same vein, recounting the magical adventures of Bink, his son Dor, and King Trent. There are trips 800 years into the past, excursions into Mundania, and battles which imperil the future of Xanth—all great fantasy stories, but a good deal more as well. For these stories of the magical land of Xanth are really stories which symbolize the unlimited possibilities of our own magical talent—the magic of our genius and the life of spirit.

The three novels in this boxed set are a wonderful introduction to the world of Piers Anthony.

More Magic of Xanth
by Piers Anthony

Since we first featured the three books in *The Magic of Xanth* series, author Piers Anthony has added three more—*Centaur Aisle, Ogre, Ogre,* and *Nightmare.* These have also now been collected in a boxed set of their own.

Xanth is a land of magic, very closely resembling the astral plane, and very much different than Mundania, which strongly resembles our own physical plane, and the limits of physical perception. In Xanth, almost anything can happen—and sooner or later in these novels, it generally does!

But the conflicts, all of which are approached with good humor and in high style, mostly revolve around the efforts of barbaric, stupid, or earthbound creatures to overrun Xanth or steal some of its magic—and that gives these stories a wonderful esoteric dimension. Story by story, we are led to a better understanding of what our proper relationship with the magic of our inner potential—and spirit—should be.

Actually, Piers Anthony did not stop writing Xanth novels with these six, although these are the only ones in boxed sets. At last count, he had written a total of nine, and rumor has it that there are still more to come. Unlike some neverending series, the Xanth books remain both enjoyable and esoterically profound.

Siddhartha
by Hermann Hesse

Siddhartha is a Brahmin youth in India who seeks the spiritual path. He therefore leaves his father's house to become a traveling ascetic, taking with him his childhood friend, Govinda.

Siddhartha is an exceptionally gifted ascetic, able to withstand the deprivations of self-denial with little trouble. But he does not find enlightenment through the life of asceticism. As he tells Govinda, "What I have so far learned from the Samanas, I could have learned more quickly and easily in every inn in a prostitute's quarters." So he leaves the ranks of the ascetics, and travels to hear the Buddha. From listening to the Buddha, he realizes what he has been searching for: knowledge of himself. But he also realizes that no teacher, even the Buddha, can give him that knowledge.

Govinda becomes a disciple of the Buddha, but Siddhartha plunges himself into the swirl of human activity, taking on a lover and becoming a merchant. He grows rich, but gradually realizes he is a stranger in the world of the average man. His real interest is discovering who he is.

At the peak of his success, he walks away from it and settles by a river. It is just an ordinary river, but to Siddhartha, it becomes the river of life. He studies its rhythms and harmonies and, by learning what the river is, he also learns who he is.

And once he has learned, finally, what he has sought after so diligently, his friend Govinda comes to him again, and Siddhartha shares what he has learned.

Siddhartha is an eloquent and moving story.

Saga of the Well World
by Jack L. Chalker

"I want to die, boy. I want to die—and I can't. Not ever. Not at all. And I want death so very much."

Varnett shook his head uncomprehendingly. "I can't figure you, Brazil. I just can't figure you."

"What do you want, Varnett?" Brazil asked, changing tone. "What would you wish for yourself?"

"I've thought a lot about that," the other replied. "I'm only 15 years old, Brazil. Just 15. My world has always been dehumanized people and cold mathematics. I'm the oldest 15 of my race, now, though. I think, perhaps, I'd like to enjoy life, enjoy a human life—and somehow make my contribution to progress. To stop this headlong rush of the human race into a Markovian hell and try to build the society they hoped would evolve from their tens of thousands of cultures and races. There's a greatness here in the Markovian Well, a potential unrealized, but great nonetheless. I'd like to see it reached, to complete the equations the Markovians couldn't."

"So would I, boy," Brazil replied earnestly. "For then I could die."

In this scrap of dialogue between one of the youngest products of creation and one of the oldest, Jack L. Chalker encapsulates the hope of the universe he has so brilliantly created in his five-novel series, *Saga of the Well World*. Nathan Brazil cannot die because it is his destiny to preserve the universe from destruction. He has lived since the beginning of the Markovian universe, and cannot die until the drama of creation is completed. And there are all kinds of cunning, devious, and selfish people, races, and societies who are all too willing to risk destroying the whole universe in order to seize control of it.

Brazil, the prototypal "wandering Jew," moves in and out of the lives of these people and societies, not always remembering who he is or what he has done in the past, but remaining a servant of the creative ideals it is his duty to protect. When we first meet Brazil, he is captain of a space freighter. But as the story of the first book, *Midnight at the Well of Souls*, unfolds, Brazil is drawn to the Well World, where a magnificent civilization once flourished and then disappeared.

The people of this ancient civilization were the Markovians, masters of the secrets of creation—including the ability to generate new forms of life and to change existing forms into totally different ones—changing, for example, a human being into a 500-pound creature who is a walrus at the upper end and a snake at the lower. Actually, Markovian science is not dead at all—it turns out to be quite active. And as this news spreads throughout the universe, the Well World, with its Well of Souls, becomes the object of war, greed, and selfishess.

The remaining four novels in the epic series—*Exile at the Well of Souls, Quest for the Well of Souls, The Return of Nathan Brazil*, and *Twilight at the Well of Souls*—chronicle these conflicts and struggles, and the central role played by Brazil in keeping life in the universe evolving as it is meant to. Indeed, it slowly becomes apparent that Brazil is not acting on his own, but as an agent of universal intelligence and order, a central feature of Markovian science. The development of new life forms, the transfer of consciousness from one form to another, and the struggle between good and evil are all regulated in an orderly fashion.

As in real life, the rules and destiny which govern these events have been laid out by divine intelligence, but the characters are allowed to stumble through their paces on their own. The outcome is not guaranteed, even though the principles of evolution are.

In this way, Chalker takes a fascinating story, endows it with a complex plot, striking characters, and surprising twists, and then uses it to convey a number of esoteric themes of importance: reincarnation, the evolution of consciousness, good versus evil, and the dualities of the personality and the soul, consciousness and matter. In general, Chalker is able to communicate these ideas more effectively in these novels than other writers have been able to in essays and treatises. This is always the beauty of excellent fiction—it lets the author take complex themes and bring them to life within a living environment of action and suspense.

Saga of the Well World is a powerful stimulus to many of the abstract faculties of the mind. These novels challenge our narrowmindedness and cultural prejudices, helping us go beyond them. Their themes are so well executed that reading them becomes a most enjoyable exercise in grasping the infinite and multidimensional nature of the universal mind—even for readers already used to working with abstract and symbolic thought. In short, this is something more than just a summer treat. It is a must for anyone interested in stretching his or her mind to embrace universal themes and ideas.

LORD OF LIGHT
by Roger Zelazny

The conflict between matter and spirit is an eternal struggle, obvious to any intelligent person who observes his own life or events in society. Theology, sociology, psychology, and philosophy deal with this conflict on their own terms. But in many ways, this struggle is best explored through good fiction.

This is exactly what Roger Zelazny's *Lord of Light* does. Condensing the many facets of the eternal battle into a few symbolic themes, Zelazny skillfully weaves them into a tapestry of plot, myth, heroism, cowardice, destruction, and triumph.

The story takes place on another planet in the far future. A few men have set themselves up as gods, borrowing freely from the Hindu pantheon, and control the world with technological mastery.

Through their machinations and advanced science, they stifle progress and create an intellectual dark age. But the Lord of Light, known as Maitreya and as Buddha, opposes them, not with superior technical power but with his philosophy and teaching, which exposes the hypocrisy and lust of the "gods" while liberating the people.

Quoting the book, "Death and Light are everywhere, always, and they begin, end, strive, attend into and upon the Dream of the Nameless that is the world, burning words within Samsara, perhaps to create a thing of beauty."

Zelazny's creation of beauty gives new life to rich Hindu myths, in a fascinating clash between light and darkness.

Forces of the Zodiac
Companions of the Soul
by Robert R. Leichtman, M.D. & Carl Japikse

Each human being is influenced constantly by a wide variety of subtle forces. Most of us, however, are largely unaware of these forces—or their impact on our lives, problems, and opportunities. As a result, we are unable to act in life as effectively as we could.

The primary way in which humanity has sought to study these invisible influences on our lives has been through the science of astrology. Unfortunately, the practice of astrology has often been cheapened by people who have used it only to speculate about the future.

Forces of the Zodiac: Companions of the Soul sets forth a brilliant new way of using astrological information. Written by Dr. Robert R. Leichtman and Carl Japikse, it is a practical guide to using the psychological and spiritual forces which are available to us to accelerate personal growth, expand our creativity, enrich relationships, strengthen leadership skills, solve problems, and seize opportunities.

According to the authors, this book is the result of six years of research, which began with the observation that certain trends, themes, and qualities influence everyone alike in each monthly sign of the zodiac—regardless of his or her natal sign. Everyone, for example, experiences a strong surge of aspiration and ambition each year when the sun is in Sagittarius—not just people born during that month.

For six years, Leichtman and Japikse intuitively studied and observed the changing forces. With their research completed, they took their findings and put them together, producing *Forces of the Zodiac.*

The book consists of a thorough description of astrological influences, what they mean to us, how to tune into them, and how we can harness them in our life. These preliminary chapters are then followed by 12 chapters of commentary describing how the forces of the 12 signs of the zodiac influence us. Each chapter explores:

• The major archetypal forces which characterize one sign of the zodiac, and their divine purpose.

• The symbolism of the sign.

• How the major forces of the sign affect the average person, the spiritual aspirant, and the advanced person.

• The challenges of the sign to parents, friends, business, society, and spiritual aspiration.

• The problems of the sign.

• The opportunities of the sign.

• How to tune into the forces of the sign.

The book concludes with a chapter about what it means to use the forces of the zodiac as "companions of the soul." In fact, "companions of the soul" sums up one of the authors' primary themes, which is to demonstrate that these forces of the zodiac are living, dynamic energies which are vital parts of the divine creative effort. As such, our soul utilizes these forces on a regular basis, both in planning the direction of our life and our current opportunities for growth and service. It regards them as its companions.

Forces of the Zodiac is a truly useful book—a book which should be our companion as we make our way through each month of the year.

The Initiation of the World

by Vera Stanley Alder

In her introduction, Vera Alder calls *The Initiation of the World* a different kind of history book than those usually found in schools—"a *golden history* which holds the key to a glorious future unfoldment."

And that is precisely what it is—a history not of wars, changes in government, and the rise and fall of empires, but rather a history of the development of the mind, the genius, and the spiritual nature of humanity. In short, easy-to-read chapters, Miss Alder tells the story of mankind's esoteric evolution.

Beginning with chapters on the growth of the mind and the plan of creation, she then proceeds to examine the significance of the following themes in our cultural and spiritual development:

- Reincarnation.
- The seven rays.
- The Hierarchy.
- The path of initiation.
- The initiations of man.
- The great world teachers.

Using these themes, she then weaves an illuminating story about the birth of national genius and the initiation of the world as a whole. The result is a very provocative and intelligent examination of the concept of brotherhood—not as an utopian ideal but as a constant thread running throughout the *real* history of mankind, the impetus of human unfoldment.

This important book is must reading for anyone seeking a truer understanding of life on this planet.

The Unfinished Autobiography
by Alice A. Bailey

For thirty-five years, Alice A. Bailey worked in close, telepathic rapport with the master Djwhal Khul, writing 25 of the most profound books on the spiritual life, psychology, healing, and cosmology ever produced— from *Initiation, Human and Solar* to *The Reappearance of the Christ*.

It is easy to assume that anyone who could produce such a monumental opus must be a virtually indestructible person. And yet the strain on Mrs. Bailey was frequently great, as she stood at the forefront of human evolution.

Her *Unfinished Autobiography* is a candid portrait of her life and work—consistently witty, intellectually stimulating, and filled with revelations. It is, after all, not just the story of her life, but also the story of her bond with Djwhal Khul and her own Master, Koot Hoomi. Yet for all the fascinating anecdotes about the Masters, the real strength of Alice Bailey's autobiography is the human dimension it brings to spiritual service. Here, she chronicles the joys and rigors of a long and busy life, and gives an inside look at the sacrifices involved in serving humanity.

It is an "unfinished" autobiography because Mrs. Bailey had envisioned four more sections. But in their place, there is fascinating material about the nature of her telepathic rapport with the Tibetan, a summary of her books, and the principles of esoteric teaching.

The Unfinished Autobiography is highly recommended.

Childhood's End
by Arthur C. Clarke

Just as the United States and Russia are about to launch the first rockets to the moon, enormous spaceships carrying "Overlords" appear over the major capitals of the world and begin issuing instructions to mankind. The Overlords do not actually appear on earth—they send their instructions through the secretary-general of the United Nations—but they back up their orders with nonviolent yet effective demonstrations of great power.

Within a few years, they achieve a dramatic improvement in the course of civilization—although not without resistance from terrorists, religious fanatics, and nationalists. But the resistance is contained, and the real work of the Overlords on earth begins—the creation of a new race of "wonder children" who represent the next step in evolution for humanity.

These children are far superior to any human being—and are even greater than the Overlords themselves. They have apparently transcended matter and are able to transmute it, which they do, in a scene of fiery transformation.

Childhood's End is a marvelously rich novel which introduces us to several significant themes: the idea that there is a Hierarchy of advanced humans who protect and guide the development of civilization and humanity; the rebelliousness of humanity toward its own destiny and purpose; and the ultimate transformation of human consciousness, leading to an entirely new race of God-like people.

This is Arthur Clarke at his best.

The Power of the Rays & Colour Meditations
by S.G.J. Ouseley

S.G.J. Ouseley has established a rightful reputation as the leading authority on the esoteric meaning and enlightened use of color. *The Power of the Rays* and *Colour Meditations* are his two most definitive statements on the subject.

Throughout both of these excellent books, Ouseley makes the point that he is referring to color as the life force symbolized by the hues of the spectrum. He leads us beyond the form of color to become aware of the quality of each color and the potent force associated with it.

These forces, he explains, can be highly useful in both meditative and healing work. In *The Power of the Rays*, he develops the "science of color healing," in which he describes the curative power of the seven major colors—and how to use them. In *Colour Meditations*, he explores the esoteric values of color and the use of these energies in meditation.

While the visualization of colors should never be considered a substitute for healing or meditative work, a true understanding of color, as presented in these two books, can be a highly useful adjunct to both healing and meditation. The key is to keep our priorities focused on establishing the right quality of consciousness, rather than the vivid image of a color.

Virtually all books written about color and color therapy are based on the work done by Ouseley and described in these books. Yet none of the books that copy Ouseley's work is as good as these.

Two Books on Symbols

The enlightened person knows that the language of every nation and people is something more than words and grammar. It is also the language of symbolism: the themes and images of its myths, heroes, religions, and civilization.

This is a language which speaks to us subconsciously, and so it is easy to miss its significance. But the intelligent person probes beyond the outer appearances of life, trying to understand the deeper significances that can be found at inner levels.

All of life is symbolic. As we learn to recognize this truth and become familiar with the symbolic language of our own culture—as well as the symbolic idiom of other important cultures throughout the world—we greatly enrich our understanding of ourselves, our neighbors, our civilization, and the other peoples of the earth.

The problem is that sometimes it is hard to separate the personal and cultural meaning of symbols. Fortunately, there are a number of excellent collections of symbols available to the reader. Two of the best are *An Illustrated Encyclopedia of Traditional Symbols* by J.C. Cooper and *A Dictionary of Symbols* by J.E. Cirlot.

Both are the work of intelligent scholarship and a thorough knowledge of cultural symbolism, making them vastly superior to the dream interpretation guides which have flooded the market recently. The entries are arranged alphabetically, making it easy to locate the meaning of symbols. In addition, the Cirlot dictionary features an index for cross referencing, and Cooper has a glossary defining unusual terms.

These are marvelous books to thumb through, reading entries at random. But the real value is to use them as guides to understand the meanings of specific symbols that arise in dreams or meditations, or are encountered in books, plays, movies, art, music, or ceremonies.

Only the ignorant person dismisses these symbols as unimportant. The intelligent individual has long since discovered the enrichment which comes from pursuing their meanings—and tapping their archetypal force. As Cooper writes:

"Symbolism is basic to the human mind; to ignore it is to suffer a serious deficiency; it is fundamental to thinking."

The very nature of symbolism, however, is multidimensional, in that any one image or theme may have many different implications and values. It is therefore dangerous to rely on just one source for the interpretation of symbols. It is for this reason that *both* of these books are recommended.

In using these two books, though, it is good to remember that symbols are not to be taken literally. The value of these two volumes is not that they make a final statement on the meaning of any symbol, but that they help *start* the thinking and interpretative process. They encourage us to put our minds to work to understand the symbolic patterns around us.

These two books will serve the thinking person well throughout a lifetime of personal investigation. They are highly recommended as cornerstones of any personal library or bookshelf.

God Always Says Yes
by Sue Sikking

"There is a great affirmative Power within every human form. There is an All-Knowing Presence within us that always says, 'Yes!' It is that something that has kept every man on the path toward some goal since the beginning of time. It is the power that fulfills our destiny, the spur to all progress."

So writes Sue Sikking in introducing the basic theme of this little gem of a book—a book about each of us, our problems, and our relationship with God. We have the power to say both yes and no to the great possibilities of our life, she explains. But regardless of what we say, the divine presence within us always says yes.

If we desire something constructive, or try to treat others fairly, the inner power of the God within us helps us attain what our heart desires. But if we fear success, or worry about what others will do to us, we are also invoking our inner power, magnifying what our heart desires.

The challenge is to break out of the ruts which trap us in downward spirals—and this is where *God Always Says Yes* shines. Mrs. Sikking offers suggestion after suggestion for breaking free from the limitation of our past, our failures, and our habits, so we may find and cultivate what she calls "a treasure in our heart."

Sue Sikking was for years the minister of one of the largest Unity churches in the country. She writes from her own rich experiences about using the power of the mind, linked with spirit, to overcome life's limitations and tragedies.

God Always Says Yes is a real treasure.

Stranger In a Strange Land
by Robert Heinlein

The stranger is Valentine Michael Smith. The strange land is Earth, where Smith, a Martian, inhabits a human body. It is hard for Smith to comprehend the strange ways of humans—strange ways such as sex, religion, and laughter. He is more at home with the customs of "grokking" and "sharing water."

The humans, of course, have just as much difficulty, even more so, understanding the ways of Smith—such as his ability to levitate, to stop objects in mid-air, and to communicate telepathically.

The effort of Smith to understand humans and the efforts of his friends to understand him create an outstanding story—consistently funny, unrelentingly satiric, and filled with brilliant insights into what it means to *expand consciousness*.

In the end, however, it is not Smith's Martian heritage that makes him a stranger in a strange land, but his rapport with humans. He taps the essence of the human experience—he groks in fullness—and seeks to share it with others, only to be rejected by those who fear their own humanity, their own divinity.

In this way, Heinlein shows us that *we* become strangers in a strange land whenever we fail to tap the fullness of our humanity or reject our mission here on earth. Of course, we could help our cause by learning to grok. And Valentine Michael Smith is just the stranger to teach us how.

Anyone who has not yet read *Stranger in a Strange Land* should not postpone doing so one more day.

The Time Quartet
by Madeleine L'Engle

It is unusual that four of the best books written recently on the conflict of good and evil are children's stories. It is likewise unusual that four of the most mind-stretching books on the fourth dimension are children's stories. It is astonishing that these are the same four books.

The Time Quartet by Madeleine L'Engle *is* unusual. And excellent. These four novels richly deserve the awards they have won and their increasing popularity.

Do not be sidetracked by the fact that these are children's books. Although unmistakeably written for children, these books delight and enlighten adults, too.

All four books—*A Wrinkle in Time, A Wind in the Door, A Swiftly Tilting Planet,* and *Many Waters*— chronicle the adventures of the Murry family, primarily Meg and Charles Wallace. Meg is unusually bright and plucky, but Charles Wallace is something else. Even at five, at the start of the novels, his vocabulary and wisdom surpass that of most adults. And he has the habit of hobnobbing with beings from other galaxies.

In all four books, the Murry children are drawn into confrontations with the *Echthros*, the presence of evil in the universe. In each tale, they find different ways of conquering the Echthros, which is icy cold and prone to ripping holes in the sky. Anyone who has actually had to deal with the force of evil will realize the depth of insight contained in these four books. Much can be learned from these simple stories.

In *A Wrinkle in Time*, the children's father is missing. He has been involved in a government experiment in *tesseracting*—traveling via the fourth dimension—and has been trapped by Echthroi (called It in this first story) on a dark planet. Charles Wallace, Meg, and her boyfriend Calvin are asked to rescue Mr. Murry—by three angels who appear in the form of dumpy but charming old ladies named Mrs. Whatsit, Mrs. Who, and Mrs. Which.

Taught to tesseract, the children manage to rescue Mr. Murry, but in the process, Charles Wallace becomes trapped by the It. It is up to Meg to return and face the evil in her young brother—icy cold and hard—and free him with a steadfast expression of love.

The theme of the redeeming value of love, and its power to defeat evil, is repeated in the second novel, *A Wind in the Door*. Charles Wallace is entering first grade and is intensely interested in mitochondria—intracellular organisms in the human body. And well he should be, for his own mitochondria are dying.

So is the universe; whole galaxies are disappearing. Once again, it is Meg, this time with the help of the cherubim Proginoskes, who must act to save her brother and the universe. Her adventures take her deep within the cells of Charles Wallace, through a form of intuitive rapport called *kything*. There, she learns the Echthroi are the problem; they are un-naming creation, stripping life of its identity.

To counter this danger, Meg learns to name creation as an act of love—a marvelous lesson in the value of selfhood and sacrifice.

The most epic of the four books is *A Swiftly Tilting Planet*, in which Charles Wallace travels back to crucial moments of history with Gaudior, a unicorn, to change the outcome of events, thus subtly averting the threat of dictatorship in the present. Meg stays behind, kything with her brother as he becomes four different people.

The plot is complex but extremely rich and powerful. Charles Wallace's primary weapon in this struggle with the Echthroi is a magical rune, which invokes the order of the heavens to stop the encroachment of evil.

Meg and Charles Wallace are grown up by the time of *Many Waters;* the action shifts to their twin brothers, Sandy and Dennys. They are "accidentally" tesseracted into the time of Noah, who is building the ark in anticipation of the "many waters." Caught up in a struggle of Biblical proportions, the twins struggle with the idea that God would actually destroy all life on earth with a flood, but gradually come to understand the underlying benevolence of seemingly incomprehensible divine acts—and discover, as their sister had before them, what it means to care. They likewise discover that neither time nor space can impede genuine love.

One of the most notable features of these stories is that the children are never saved by divine intervention; they triumph because they *learn* in the face of crisis, with divine help. This is a basic lesson of enlightenment.

It is also refreshing to encounter books in which intelligence and genius are treated with great respect and understanding. *The Time Quartet* is children's literature at its finest.

The Fantasy Stories
of George MacDonald

A masterpiece of art is often very simple—a few well-placed brushstrokes that capture the essence of beauty and provoke deep reflection. A masterpiece of fantasy is frequently much the same. It takes a common human situation, puts in a dream-like, allegorical, or even mythic setting, and thereby fires our imagination with new insight and a deeper appreciation of human nature.

George MacDonald was an early master of fantasy. C.S. Lewis considered him his mentor. J.R.R. Tolkein and Charles Williams both paid tribute to the "power and beauty" of his writings. In this boxed set, all of MacDonald's short fantasy stories are presented in four volumes—*The Golden Key, The Gray Wolf, The Light Princess,* and *The Wise Woman.* For those who love fantasy, these four books will be a real treasure, for MacDonald richly deserves the title "master." His stories evoke the full power of fantasy and allegory at its best, whether in a story depicting the fearsome nature of lust and greed such as "The Gray Wolf" or a tale of esoteric truth such as "The Castle."

As Madeleine L'Engle put it, "George MacDonald is the grandfather of us all—all of us who struggle to come to terms with truth through fantasy. I am delighted that these wonderful stories are going to be available to a world which is in dire need of their message."

The Fantasy Stories of George MacDonald is a wonderful boxed set to curl up with and be transported into the inner dimensions of the human imagination.

Scars of the Soul
by Mary Anne Woodward

Edgar Cayce was a remarkable psychic who, over a span of 40 years, gave almost 15,000 readings in a trance state, the majority of them for people with serious physical illnesses. Through these readings, he was able to discern the inner causes of disease and made an immense contribution to our understanding of the true nature of sickness and health.

Cayce did not view illness on just the physical level. To him, many physical ailments were the direct result of character flaws and defects carried over from earlier lifetimes. These he discussed in terms of *karma*—the esoteric principle of consequences or continuity. Quite simply, we carry the good and bad issues of our character with us as we make our life along the path. As we reinvest the good in new applications of our skills and talents, it grows and becomes more abundant. It promotes good health. Conversely, as we repeatedly indulge in the bad, and fail to transform it into something more spiritual, it cuts its groove in our character more deeply. Sooner or later, it restricts our health—and may even threaten our livingness.

Cayce referred to the deeper, more malignant "grooves" etched in our character as "scars of the soul"—not that they are actually of the soul, but that they obscure the light of the soul from shining into our character. Inspired by this phrase and her lifelong study of Cayce, Mary Anne Woodward has put together a new book on Cayce, karma, and holistic healing, aptly titled *Scars of the Soul*.

In many ways, this new book is a companion volume to Ms. Woodward's earlier book, *Edgar Cayce's Story of Karma*. In other ways, however, it is more specifically focused, and filled with valuable insights into the origin of disease.

The first few chapters are used to explain the concept of karma and how karmic trends develop from life to life. The meat of the book, however, is the third chapter, which covers more than half the text and presents case after case in which Cayce commented on the karmic antecedents of illnesses.

The range of diseases on which Cayce commented is truly impressive. The cases Ms. Woodward chose to examine begin with cancer and make their way through stroke, paralysis, diabetes, tuberculosis, arthritis, asthma, acne, allergies, anemia, birth defects, epilepsy, multiple sclerosis, Parkinson's, alcoholism, and even accidents and homosexuality. It is fascinating to read the way in which Cayce handled this wide diversity of illnesses. Whenever possible, he devoted the majority of his comments to practical steps which could be taken to alleviate the pain and suffering of the diseased condition, but he likewise attempted to show as clearly as possible the underlying psychological problems which gave rise to the difficulty—and what could be done to correct them.

A case of epilepsy, for instance, is traced back to a lifetime (probably a series of lives) in which the individual lusted to control and dominate others for his own self-aggrandizement, almost to the point of possession. A case of cancer is traced to a lifetime in which the person mocked the suffering of others—Christians who were being persecuted for their faith.

In the first case, the person was trapped in the disease; no tangible improvement was reported. In the second, a conscious effort was made to alter the character flaws that induced the karma, and the "incurable cancer" was cured.

Many of the cases examined in this book are less life threatening, yet nonetheless instructive. In one in particular, a young man was suffering from multiple sclerosis and eventually went blind. Cayce chided him for being selfish and filled with malice and told him the outcome of his physical condition would depend on inner changes: "When the body becomes so self-satisfied, so self-centered as to renounce, refuse, or does not change its attitude, so long as there is hate, malice, injustice.... there cannot be healing to that condition of this body....What would the body be healed for? That it might add to its own selfishness? Then it had better remain as it is."

It is in comments such as these that the real value of *Scars of the Soul* lies. Time after time, Cayce hits the important themes of health squarely on target. It is clear that he understood that it is not a condition from 5,000 years ago which prevents us from enjoying good health today, even though it may have cast the pattern for our problem. It is our unwillingness to grow and become a mature person, by changing our character, that keeps us trapped in ill health—even for 5,000 years!

The one weak area of the book is the final chapter on the use of meditation to change karmic patterns; the description of meditation is too simplistic and filled with cliches of spiritual growth to be of much real help. But if this last chapter is skipped, most people will find *Scars of the Soul* enlightening.

Occult Medicine Can Save Your Life
by C. Norman Shealy, M.D.

"There is a magic in medicine, there always has been—and this is why medical miracles are a recognized and well-documented aspect of professional practice and medical care. Perhaps that magic is love-energy, perhaps it's faith—for certainly no patient has ever been helped or cured or healed unless he has had faith in what his doctor is doing for him. In any case, the doctor's task today is to put that magic—that faith—back into medicine where it belongs, to learn to make the miracles available for the patient when nothing else can help!"

So writes C. Norman Shealy, M.D. in *Occult Medicine Can Save Your Life*—a thorough evaluation of non-medical forms of healing and therapy, from acupuncture and etheric surgery to psychic diagnosis, spiritual healing, and astrology. Shealy's goal is to alert the reader to ways in which these "occult" or metaphysical practices can be used together with modern medicine, to speed the healing process.

Along the way, Dr. Shealy also frankly discusses the limitations of some practices of conventional medicine, especially the use of drugs and surgery. He writes eloquently of the holistic approach to health.

Dr. Shealy is founding president of the American Holistic Medical Association and founder of the world-famous Pain and Health Rehabilitation Center in Springfield, Missouri. *Occult Medicine Can Save Your Life* is must reading for anyone interested in the full meaning of health.

The Secret Life of the Unborn Child
by Thomas Verny, M.D.

The world of the unborn child is like a different dimension to us—dark, mysterious, something we cannot directly participate in. And most adults treat it as such. They regard the unborn fetus as unfeeling, unknowing, and unconscious.

Thomas Verny, M.D. has compiled an amazing amount of research that convincingly suggests that this just is not true. According to Dr. Verny, unborn children are:

- Capable of learning.
- Able to warn parents and doctors of medical problems they may not be aware of.
- Able to hear and respond to voices and sounds—even music.
- Able to distinguish between pleasant, classical music and discordant music such as hard rock.
- Sensitive to the feelings of their parents.
- Capable of responding to love.

These findings and more are the results of six years of study of unborn and newly-born children by psychiatrist Verny. They are compiled in his remarkable new book, *The Secret Life of the Unborn Child*.

This is an important book, not just for would-be parents but for anyone interested in understanding the nature of consciousness, the structure of our personal psychology, and the psychic capacities of the human being. Reading this book may also be a startling revelation for anyone who has struggled with confusing conflicts, likes and dislikes, and fears. It is amazing how many of these problems can actually be imprinted *prior to birth.*

Dr. Verny tells his story with charm and style, spicing the book with marvelous anecdotes such as the story of conductor Boris Brott who, early in his career, found that he often knew the cello parts of certain pieces he was conducting sight unseen. This fascinated him, so he told his mother, a professional cellist. She asked him to name the pieces in which this had happened. He did—and they all turned out to be pieces she had been rehearsing *while she was pregnant with Boris!* He had not only heard the music his mother was practicing, but had memorized every detail of it.

The real value of this book, however, lies not in its anecdotes but in its revelations and implications. One of the most important points Dr. Verny makes, for example, is that the unborn child *is* alive and aware of its environment. It is aware of the thoughts and feelings of its parents and other influences even before actual sensory organs have been developed in the fetus. In fact, the character of the new-born child is strongly influenced by the thoughts and feelings of the parents, especially the mother, during the entire time of pregnancy. Dr. Verny recounts case after case of children growing up with feelings of rejection because they were unwanted pregnancies.

On the other hand, he also presents strong evidence that babies who are praised and loved while still in utero become well-adjusted children and adults.

Although Dr. Verny does not specifically discuss these phenomena in terms of psychic communication, it is clear that the perceptions of the unborn child are psychic. In particular, he states that the unborn child is very sensitive to deep-seated patterns of parental emotion.

In this manner, *The Secret Life of the Unborn Child* presents a wealth of evidence that the psychic environment in which we live has a strong influence in shaping our conciousness. It stands to reason that if psychic influences are so strong on the unborn child, they must also be powerful factors on us after we are born.

In personal conversations with Dr. Verny, he takes this theme further than he dared to in print. He is personally convinced that the unborn child is psychically aware what its parents think about it, their general emotional state, and the major events going on in the "outside world."

He is also convinced that the unborn child is influenced by past lives, and reports that young children will often consciously remember episodes from earlier lives up to the age of four.

Even though these findings are not reported in *The Secret Life of the Unborn Child*, Dr. Verny does make a strong case for them indirectly, stating that science can no longer ignore the evidence of an "extraneurological memory system" and "sympathetic" communication. In this way, he shatters one of the great mental blocks of science—the belief that consciousness is grounded exclusively in the physical system.

The Secret Life of the Unborn Child is a study of the first nine months of human life, but it is much more than this as well. It is a study of the basis of human consciousness and its psychic nature, a landmark book which deserves to be read by everyone interested in knowing more about how we think, feel, and learn.

Far Memory
by Joan Grant

"Far memory" is the ability to recall one's earlier lifetimes with as much clarity and vividness as one might recall an episode from 20 years ago in this lifetime. Joan Grant has an exceptional talent for far memory—a talent she developed as a young adult. Then, a "chance" encounter with four Egyptian scarabs brought a number of specific lifetimes into unusually sharp and complete focus, leading to the writing of seven novels which are, in fact, recollections of earlier lives she has led, from ancient Egypt to Renaissance Italy, from thousands of years ago in America to the beginnings of the Roman Empire.

The best known of these novels, *Winged Pharaoh*, became an immediate bestseller when first published in 1937—and still remains immensely popular today, fifty years later, as do the other novels which were subsequently released.

Far Memory is Joan's autobiography. In it, Joan tells the story of her childhood and young adult life, and how she came to develop her intuitive skills and write her novels. It is a fascinating, even breathtaking story to read, as she recounts her adventures as a high-spirited child, the shock of losing her fiance through an accident, encounters with H.G. Wells, Aleister Crowley, and Sir Oliver Lodge, and, ultimately, the unfoldment of her amazing skills. In many ways, Joan's present life is as stirring as any earlier one.

Far Memory is a joy to read—and is filled with marvelous descriptions of what it means to develop real psychic talent.

Magister Ludi
by Hermann Hesse

The Glass Bead Game is a sophisticated mental encounter played by the finest minds of the 25th century. The game draws on all human knowledge, all facets of culture, and unifies it, revealing the underlying harmony of the universal mind—and the capacity of the noble human mind to tap it and interact with it.

Joseph Knecht is a brilliant student who rises to become "Magister Ludi"—the master of the Glass Bead Game. Yet Knecht is disturbed by the conventions of the game. In an effort to cultivate pure knowledge—pure culture and pure science—the game players have become oddly detached from society. They have fallen victim to the glamour of the ivory tower, believing that knowledge exists for its own sake, rather than to serve human and divine evolution.

Ultimately, Knecht relinquishes his post as master of the Game, forced by his own destiny to return to an active life. And in so doing, he demonstrates what it means to be alive in the world. We must have knowledge, but we must act on the knowledge we have, and serve life. If we train our mind sufficiently, we can gain archetypal knowledge—knowledge of the basic patterns of all creation. But once we know these things, we must activate them and translate them into achievements which help humanity and God.

Magister Ludi is a powerful novel. It sets before us a grand vista of what the mind can become, then teaches us what it means for anyone—and humanity as a whole—to grow.

YOUR POWER TO BE
by J. Sig Paulson

"The greatest power in the universe is the power to be! It expresses itself in every created thing. A drop of water, a blade of grass, a planet, a star, a dog, a cat, a bird, are all expressions of the power to be. It is in man that the power to be finds its greatest expression and its greatest potential....Man is an instrument capable of infinite expansion as he awakens to his true identity and accepts his place in the divine scheme of things."

So writes J. Sig Paulson in *Your Power To Be*, one of the most practical books in print on putting the power of spirit to work in our life. Paulson, a Unity minister in Texas, chides the churches for failing to teach their members about the spiritual light within themselves and what it means to express it through acts of love and wisdom. He then goes on to remedy the situation, presenting a drill in self-realization followed by a thorough description of our 13 powers to be—light, faith, will, understanding, imagination, enthusiasm, love, authority, wisdom, joy, strength, forgiveness, and life.

As Paulson puts it, *Your Power To Be* is a book for "the spiritually adventurous, those who are ready to walk the largely uncharted paths of their own souls." And what a great adventure it is! In a very real sense, it is an adventure into light itself—an adventure into the inner realms of human *and* divine consciousness and what can be done with it, to improve the quality of our lives and better serve God.

Your Power To be is a book which is filled with light.

The Pleasantries of the Incredible Nasrudin
by Idries Shah

Nasrudin was court jester to Tamerlane, a Persian emperor during the fourteenth century. His wise jests—or foolish wisdom—became legendary, and people throughout the Middle East soon were telling Nasrudin stories. They have not stopped since.

Along the way, many of these stories have become enriched with esoteric insights and overtones, making them not only funny stories to tell, but thought-provoking tales to ponder on, reflectively or meditatively.

A good Nasrudin story is a slippery delight; just when you think you have figured out its meaning, you find it has at least a dozen other interpretations, all equally significant. Because of this, Nasrudin stories are an excellent tool for stretching the imagination—as well as the intuition.

Idries Shah has collected the best of the Nasrudin stories and added a few of his own. Here are some:

Nasrudin went to the shop of a man who stocked all kinds of bits and pieces.

"Have you got nails?" he asked.

"Yes."

"And leather, good leather?"

"Yes."

"And twine?"

"Yes."

"And dye?"

"Yes."

"Then why, for Heaven's sake, don't you make a pair of boots?"

A Sampling of Nasrudin

Nasrudin was sitting among the branches of a tree, sniffing the blossoms and sunning himself. A traveller asked him what he was doing there.

"Climbing the Great Pyramid."

"You are nowhere near a pyramid. And there are four ways up a pyramid: one by each face. That is a tree!"

"Yes," said Nasrudin. "But it's much more fun like this, don't you think? Birds, blossoms, zephyrs, sunshine. I hardly think I could have done better."

A philosopher, having made an appointment to dispute with Nasrudin, called and found him away from home.

Infuriated, he picked up a piece of chalk and wrote "Stupid Oaf" on Nasrudin's gate.

As soon as he got home and saw this, Nasrudin rushed to the philosopher's house.

"I had forgotten," he said, "that you were to call. And I apologize for not being home. Of course, I remembered the appointment as soon as I saw that you had left your name on my door."

Nasrudin's wife heard a tremendous thump outdoors, and ran to investigate.

"Nothing to worry about," said Nasrudin, "It was only my cloak which fell to the ground."

"What, and made a noise like that?"

"Yes, I was inside it at the time."

The Chronicles of Narnia
by C.S. Lewis

Narnia is a magical land inhabited by talking animals and trees, powerful evil, magic, and spiritual forces. Four children enter Narnia through a huge wardrobe closet and become entangled in the struggles of Narnia—the struggle of the power of good to triumph over evil.

The seven books in *The Chronicles of Narnia* are often thought to be a classic of children's fantasy, and they certainly can be read at that level. But Lewis wrote these tales for adults as well—adults with eyes that see and ears that hear.

The chronicles are really an ingenious fable of the magic of divine order and the redeeming power of spirit, as it is embodied in the form of a Christ-like lion, Aslan. In order to fulfill an ancient prophecy, Aslan sacrifices himself for the children and allows himself to be slain in their stead—only to resurrect himself and become the central presence of these tales.

The adventures of Narnia continue, each illustrating an important facet of our personal struggles to live up to our divine potential, until the final book, in which the inhabitants enter a stable where Aslan is said to reside. Inside, each finds what he has created in his expectations. Those who have lived an illusion find their illusions, but those who have learned to see spiritually find a wonderful new land. And from inside the stable, they see that Narnia is ceasing to be.

All spiritual adults will treasure these marvelous and magical stories.

The Call to the Heights
by Geoffrey Hodson

In ancient times, spiritual instruction was given in mystery schools or temples. Today, even though such schools do not exist physically, the same kind of instruction is available—to anyone who answers "the call to the heights."

This is the basic message of Geoffrey Hodson's book, *The Call To The Heights*, quite possibly the most comprehensive of all the books this great clairvoyant wrote. In it, he outlines with clarity the steps involved in treading the spiritual path and opening the doorway to illumination.

Even though the mystery schools exist only at inner levels now, Hodson makes it very clear that they are more accessible than ever. He then proceeds to explain what we must do to discover our own connections to these inner sources. In specific, he describes the changes we must make in order to respond to the call to the heights—the pitfalls and glamours to avoid and the qualities to be acquired. In presenting these ideas, Hodson manages to convey a great deal of esoteric insight about the rays, discipleship, and initiation.

The result is a thoroughly modern explanation of the ancient wisdom—a rare and important achievement. But Hodson does not content himself with personal growth. Some of the best chapters are those he devotes to describing the nature of the emerging global consciousness which attends spiritual growth. He points out how important it is for each of us to become a world disciple.

This is a "call" none of us should ignore.

The Gift of Healing
by Ambrose & Olga Worrall

"The great healing power of the Holy Spirit is around us and available to us in church, in our homes, in a taxicab or a gasoline station or a hospital room—wherever the need is, one can reach out to this power. If we cannot touch the undying flame, we can, in any case, draw near its Divine warmth that reshapes and rebuilds and restores."

So write Ambrose and Olga Worrall in *The Gift of Healing*, a remarkable chronicle of their life experiences as the two best-known spiritual healers in America. It is a story of hope and the healing power of spiritual love—probably the best personal story of healing in print today.

Ambrose and Olga Worrall were responsible for the healing of thousands of people through the use of their gift over a 50-year period. In addition, Olga founded the New Life Clinic in Baltimore and participated in dozens of scientific experiments that proved beyond any doubt that spiritual healing does work and can produce amazing results.

This new, memorial edition includes a moving afterword by Robert R. Leichtman, M.D., who served on the healing team of the New Life Clinic with Olga.

The Gift of Healing is an exciting book to read, not only for its genuine insights into healing, but also for the descriptions of the Worralls' psychic abilities. It leads us into new understanding.

As the Worralls put it, "Spiritual healing, like all healing, is only a technique for achieving wholeness, and all wholeness is of God."

The Secret Path

by Paul Brunton

"True vision is a tremendous experience, not a set of theories. No man who has lived through even a temporary spiritual experience is ever likely to forget it."

So writes Paul Brunton in *The Secret Path*, his remarkable commentary on the process of contacting our Overself or soul, and how this contact enriches our life. After several years of being out of print, this classic is now available in a new edition—and deservedly so.

Paul Brunton was one of the first-rate thinkers of the 20th century—an excellent writer who tapped the inner reservoirs of spirit and then described what he had learned in his many books. But he did not write for the mystic; he wrote instead for the average intelligent person who is caught up in the struggle to make the world a better place in which to live and work and prosper—in particular, for men and women of business, practical affairs, and worldly responsibilities.

The Secret Path is written very much in this spirit, as a guide which is meant to reveal the power of the soul to replenish our physical, mental, and spiritual strength, thereby renewing us for the tasks and challenges of daily life. It is designed to lead us into a direct, not a theoretical, relationship with our real self.

Indeed, one of the continuing themes of *The Secret Path* is its emphasis on self-transformation. Over and over again, Brunton stresses the power of spirit to change our habits, thoughts, and attitudes for the better—and shows us how. This is one of those rare books which *can* change lives.

And the Devil
Will Drag You Under
by Jack L. Chalker

Suppose the universe is actually nothing more than a vast laboratory experiment created by a group of unimaginably powerful beings—and that all the laws of physics and human behavior are just the creation of the Department of Probabilities of a celestial university, as part of a research project. And suppose that earth is about to be destroyed by a collision with an asteroid. This is the premise of *And The Devil Will Drag You Under*.

Mac Walters and Jill McCullough are two humans recruited by the "supervisor" of earth to save the planet from destruction. Their mission is to travel to five alternate universes and steal five magic jewels, presumably so the supervisor can save earth.

Each of the five universes is a different experiment. In one, divine law and justice are immediate, painful, and automatic. In another, there are no rules; those with the strongest minds and wills rule everyone else. As Mac and Jill journey through these strange dimensions, they learn to adapt—and they also learn how important free will, individuality, and a sense of inner morality are. Ultimately, of course, Mac and Jill are successful in obtaining the five jewels. It is then that we learn that the "supervisor" is not what he claimed to be, as the genuine order of the universe acts swiftly and effectively to prevent him from grabbing control of the whole system.

And The Devil Will Drag You Under is top notch science fiction, the work of a highly talented author.

The Boy Who Saw True

Most diaries given to children as Christmas presents become treasure troves of their deepest feelings and most private secrets, and the diary published as *The Boy Who Saw True* is no exception. Rather, it is the boy who wrote it who was exceptional.

"Seeing true" is the capacity to see clairvoyantly, and this delightful book is the actual diary of a small boy with clairvoyant gifts growing up in Victorian England. Published anonymously in 1953 after the author's death as an adult, *The Boy Who Saw True* records the trials and tribulations of growing up psychic in a family with absolutely no appreciation for psychic abilities.

"I was too in the dumps to write my diary last night," the lad reports on Feb. 19, 1885. "When Mildred and I came back from Arnold's where we'd been asked to tea, we went to speak to mamma in the morning room, and I saw Uncle Willie sitting in papa's chair and smiling at us. And just then papa came back from bizzness, and after he had kissed us all, was going to sit down, when I cried, 'Don't sit there, Uncle Willie is sitting in that chair.' And mamma looked all funny, and said, 'I rarely don't know what we're going to do with that child,' and papa said, very cross, 'What *are* you talking about, boy? Why, your Uncle Willie has been dead these two years.' Then he told Mildred to take me upstairs at once."

Only slowly does the boy come to learn that not everyone can see spirits, auras, gnomes, fairies, and other psychic realities as he can—in fact, almost no one can. He also learns not to talk about what he sees clairvoyantly with his family members, who only ridicule or punish him for it. Instead, he pours his observations into his diary. The result is a truly remarkable chronicle of genuine psychic gifts and their development.

The entries were edited by the author shortly before his death, but have been left in their original form, complete with the spelling errors, grammar mistakes, and innocent gaffes a small boy would make. This also preserves the full spirit, charm, and humanity with which they were written.

And this is one of the great features of the book: it is not a dry textbook on psychic realities or the spiritual life, but a vivid, *living* account of life as seen through penetrating, clear-seeing eyes. It is both entertaining to read and profoundly insightful—a rare combination indeed.

As the boy realizes that no one in his family can understand him, he builds a strong bond with his Uncle Willie and his grandfather, both of whom are in spirit. They comfort him in his bewilderment, guide him through several crises, and introduce him to some basic ideas about the inner planes.

At one point, for example, the boy asks his grandfather why his grandmother never comes to visit as he does. "And he said something about spirits getting thought-bound like birds getting egg-bound, and made us laugh because it seemed such a funny thing to say. He told us that while the grandmater was still on earth, she reckoned, same as a lot of people do, that she and a few others who thought exactly as she did were the only people what were going to be saved. 'And now,' said grandpa, 'she lives in a world of thoughts which she and others have created with their own fallacious convictions."

Slowly, the boy's world expands. He is assigned a tutor who is impressed by his psychic abilities and begins to study them with an open mind. He encourages the boy to conduct various experiments psychically, and this provides some of the most interesting material in the book.

Later, the boy makes the acquaintance, psychically, of an "Elder Brother" and some of his disciples, who teach the lad about his psychic gifts and the spiritual life. These teachings are also recorded in the diary, providing an unusual glimpse into the support and instruction given by a Master to a spiritual aspirant.

Perhaps most significantly, however, this book is a candid account of the problems closed-mindedness can create, especially in raising children. Talented children often have a difficult time in growing up, because their talents separate them from other children and many adults. This is particularly true when the talents are psychic gifts. Many people are so sure of their own opinions that they instantly reject all evidence to the contrary, even when the evidence comes from the observations of an honest little boy.

Truly, the heroes of this book are the ones who help the boy to understand himself, his talents, and the world around him. They stand out clearly from those with closed minds, who constantly fail to accept the lad for what he is—or even try to understand him.

The Boy Who Saw True is an important contribution to psychic literature. It is highly recommended—to parents, to children, and to everyone interested in the inner dimensions of life.

Thought-Forms
by Annie Besant & C.W. Leadbeater

"Each definite thought produces a double effect—a radiating vibration and a floating form," write the authors of *Thought-Forms*. "The thought itself appears first to clairvoyant sight as a vibration in the mental body, and this may be either simple or complex."

Examining these thought-forms and vibrations, both in their simple and their complex arrangements, is the purpose of *Thought-Forms*, unquestionably the most authoritative statement on the subject in print. Annie Besant and C.W. Leadbeater were both outstanding clairvoyants in the early decades of this century, and this book is a record of their observations of the nature of thoughts and emotions.

One of the great virtues of this book is that it is richly illustrated, in color, with drawings based on the observations of the authors. In addition to reading about the difference between grief and joy, for instance, we can see it graphically for ourselves.

The insights presented in this way are both stunning and illuminating. The authors examine the meaning of color and the vibratory nature of thought, then go on to case after case example of the psychic nature of affection, devotion, anger, fear, greed, and sympathy, as well as a detailed examination of the kind of thought-forms produced during meditation, those produced by healing or kind thoughts directed at others, and those generated by music.

All in all, this is one of the most fascinating books on clairvoyance in print.

The Brotherhood
of Angels & Men
by Geoffrey Hodson

Angels have always been a topic of fascination to men and women, especially those who have embarked on the spiritual path. But most of what has been written about angels has been idle speculation—and outright invention. Some people believe, for example, that human beings become angels after they die. Others would teach us to fear angels, making them into divine accountants who record our sins in preparation for a final and irrevocable judgment.

In point of fact, angels are part of a separate line of evolution—the deva kingdom—which embraces a vast spectrum of consciousness from primitive nature spirits to advanced archangels. Like humans, there are many types and grades of angels. But unlike humans, angels do not incarnate directly through form. Their work and destiny differ from the roles played by men and women.

Despite these differences, men and angels are meant to share the work they do with one another. For many eons, however, this has not been possible; the materialistic tendency of mankind to become absorbed in ignorance, selfishness, and negativity has made it impossible for the angel kingdom to draw near. Still, the ideal of a "brotherhood of angels and men" remains active, and it was to promote this ideal that the remarkable book by Geoffrey Hodson, *The Brotherhood of Angels and Men*, was written.

According to Hodson, one of the most gifted clairvoyants of the 20th century, the text of the book was dictated to him by the angel Bethelda, in the hope of inspiring men and women to learn the true nature of angels and how to communicate effectively with them. Whether written by angel or by man, *The Brotherhood of Angels and Men* is a lovely and inspiring book to read. It teaches us not only about angels, but also about ourselves—and how to strive for the highest, the noblest, and the best within us and life.

Bethelda begins by describing the purposes served by angels. "Behind every phenomenon you will find a member of our race. Our position in nature is closely akin to that of the engineer; he is not the force himself; he directs it, and as his constant care and oversight are essential to the efficient running of the machine, so the angels, or devas, are essential to the efficient running of the great machine of nature, as well as each individual engine of which it is composed, from atom to archangel."

In specific, seven great divisions of angels are presented:

Angels of power, who direct and release divine energies.

Angels of healing, who seek to aid mankind in healing illness.

Guardian angels of the home, who vivify and protect the noble elements of family life.

Angels who build, embodying archetypal ideas.

Angels of nature, who oversee the distribution of divine forces through nature.

Angels of music, who translate the radiance of God into sound.

Angels of beauty, who preserve and enrich the divine vision.

Because mankind is also interested in these activities, it is both reasonable and beneficial for men and women to learn to interact with angels. But striking up a relationship with angelic forces is not the same as building a friendship with another human being. In fact, Bethelda is quite insistent that close personal contact with angels should not be the goal of human and angelic interaction. With this injunction clearly stated, the angel then proceeds to describe how a bridge of communication can be established between humans and angels, and to suggest a number of invocations which can be used in contacting angels.

The angel also describes the proper posture for communicating with angels—and this is the real heart of the book. In nine brilliant chapters, Bethelda touches the essence of excellence, patience, education, joy, vision, thoroughness, unity, and the path. Each of these chapters is a poetic meditation on one of these nine qualities. Swiftly and clearly, we are led to a deeper realization of these archetypal forces—and, if we read in the right spirit, we learn what it means to be in communion with the brotherhood of angels.

This is an important book, one which can be read many times over, always renewing our sense of dedication to the divine plan. As Bethelda puts it:

"The Angels ask from you, not worship—for that would be inappropriate—but love. The power of our prayers will be enhanced by being offered up with yours; your lives will be enriched by the answer to our common act of praise. Our sphere of usefulness to God will be enlarged by sharing yours; your lives will be enriched, your world made glad, by the inauguration of the Brotherhood of Angels and of Men."

From Bethlehem to Calvary
by Alice A. Bailey

The initiations of the spiritual path are, by their very nature, a great mystery—one which is often confusing, yet usually quite appealing, to the spiritual aspirant. As a result, a lot of nonsense and misinformation has been written about initiation, and many people have formed fanciful beliefs of what it entails.

From Bethlehem to Calvary is a very practical commentary on the mysteries of initiation—one that all spiritual aspirants will find extremely helpful. Alice Bailey compares the five major initiations of the spiritual path with five important events in the life of the Christ—thereby helping us better understand the symbolic meaning of these episodes as well as the true meaning of initiation. The five initiations are:

1. The Birth at Bethlehem.
2. The Baptism in the Jordan.
3. The Transfiguration.
4. The Crucifixion.
5. The Resurrection and Ascension.

One by one, these episodes from the life of Christ are examined from the perspective of how Jesus was initiated into a greater range of understanding, enlightenment, and service. But this is not really a book about Jesus—it is a book about each of us who aspires to initiation. It is written to be used by the spiritual aspirant to understand the changes which must be made in his or her life in order to serve a larger role in the life of mankind.

From Bethlehem To Calvary is an outstanding book.

The Sea Priestess
by Dion Fortune

Vivien Le Fay Morgan is a practicising initiate of the Hermetic Path who is able to transform herself into her namesake, Morgan Le Fay, the sea priestess of Atlantis, servant of Isis, and foster daughter of Merlin.

Wilfred Maxwell is an asthmatic young man who falls in love with Morgan and agrees to serve as her priest in a series of magical experiments meant to harness the power of Isis—Isis the Veiled, the Great Mother of Nature, rather than Isis Unveiled, the Heavenly Mother.

What ensues is a magical evocation of the magnetic workings of nature and the orderly intelligence of the planet earth—and how men and women fit into this grand evolutionary scheme. And in the course of exploring and discovering the magnetic relationships of nature, they also explore the relationship between man and woman, male and female, as well as the underlying divine archetypes of human sexuality.

The Sea Priestess is an amazingly rich novel which stirs the imagination and deepens our appreciation of the power of magic. It is filled with brilliant insights into human psychology—a particular interest of Dion Fortune—and reveals the way in which our character is built up out of the interplay between male and female elements.

In the end, however, it becomes the story of why Isis is veiled—and what it means to behold the great Goddess unveiled, in Her supreme glory.

The Sea Priestess is a marvelous novel, a masterpiece of magical fiction. It is highly recommended.

Memories, Dreams, Reflections
by Carl G. Jung

Dreams and the content of the deepest regions of our unconscious minds are subjects of intense interest to many people, especially those who are pursuing greater self-awareness. In recent years, many books have been written about dreams, but almost all have been disappointing.

The one exception is *Memories, Dreams, Reflections*, which does not actually purport to be a book about dreams. It is the memoir of the brilliant psychologist Carl G. Jung, written just prior to his death in 1961. Nonetheless, since Jung made a career out of being an intrepid explorer of the subconscious and unconscious, this is a book which teaches us more about dreams than any other book in print.

Jung is absolutely candid in exploring his inner life, even from a very early age. In this way, he shows how his thinking developed—and what it means to lead an examined, intelligent life. He relates his inner life to the outer events which normally fill so much space in an autobiography, but in the case of this book, it is the inner drama that keeps us reading, unable to set the book down, not the outer.

Memories, Dreams, Reflections is one of the most important books of our century. In it, Jung not only summarizes the major discoveries he made in his career in psychology, but also sets a new standard for the intelligent examination of inner phenomena. He makes it quite clear that the "self" is the only reasonable laboratory for psychological investigation.

The Arthurian Saga
by Mary Stewart

The legend of King Arthur and his great magician Merlin has been popular in every age. Each generation produces new versions of this romantic tale, for the themes of the lives of Arthur and Merlin are as fascinating and informative as they are timeless.

Mary Stewart's four-book set on Arthur and Merlin conveys fresh insight into the meaning of these heroes to our culture. It begins with *The Crystal Cave*, continues with *The Hollow Hills* and *The Last Enchantment*, and reaches its conclusion in *The Wicked Day*.

At first, the stories focus on Merlin, from the turmoil of his childhood through his training to be a magician to the fulfillment of his destiny. In this sense, these books are the story of a man who slowly comes to understand his affinity to magical forces and how God chooses to use him to aid his king. Those who have felt drawn by higher forces beyond their control will be able to identify with these elements of Merlin's life.

Merlin, of course, foretells both the rise and fall of Arthur, and fate, destiny, and prophecy are powerful themes coursing through all four books. Gradually, however, the emphasis shifts from the magical to the human, until in *The Wicked Day*, Arthur learns the full meaning of his destiny:

"We have let ourselves be blinded by prophecy. We have lived under the edge of doom....But fate is made by men, not gods. Our own follies, not the gods, foredoom us. The gods are spirits; they work by men's hands, and there are men brave enough to stand up and say: *I am a man; I will not.*"

The Greater Trumps
by Charles Williams

Good fiction has the opportunity to focus on life in ways that no other form of writing can. It can build a structure of symbols that speak directly to the reader's subconscious; if it is inspired fiction, it can raise this structure of symbols to allegorical or even archetypal levels.

By its nature, good fiction is meant to build suspense, thereby entertaining us. It is therefore the ideal medium for examining the nature of crisis and its power to help us grow—or destroy us. It can be almost poetic and introspective at times, action-oriented at others.

The very best fiction, of course, creates a world of its own, and lures the reader into its mythos. Such novels are animated by the very power of their inspiration—the essence of the author's insight or inspiration.

Every once in a while, a novel is written which seems to be animated by something even greater than the author's imagination. As the story unfolds, it kindles a momentum and sense of drama which carry the reader to a transcendent view of life.

The Greater Trumps by Charles Williams is such a book. It is not an ordinary novel with an esoteric theme; it is as close to an "archetypal experience" as a piece of fiction could be.

On the surface, The Greater Trumps is a story about the Tarot. The Tarot is a system of symbolism and archetypal design—a system of creative force which holds many keys to the inner patterns of our life.

In The Greater Trumps, the Tarot comes to life in an

unusual way. Henry, a young man of gypsy descent, and his family have made a study of the Tarot for many years. They have gone so far as to create a set of sculptures of the major Arcana, which they position on a table in an inner sanctum of their home. These Tarot images are almost alive and can be moved in patterns which generate actual changes in physical events.

Lothair Coningsby owns a Tarot deck of unusual power—quite possibly the original Tarot deck from which all others descended. Henry discovers the existence of this deck through Lothair's daughter Nancy, with whom Henry falls in love.

Nancy demonstrates an unusual ability to work with the Tarot. Henry determines to steal the magical deck from her father. When his scheme is frustrated, he plots murder, using the the forces of the Tarot to manipulate the natural elements, creating a fierce blizzard on Christmas day.

The plot backfires, of course, and both families are threatened by total destruction—and quite possibly the whole human race is in danger, too. But the danger exists only in the minds and hearts of those who misunderstand the true power of life. For Nancy's aunt, Sybil, is a woman of unusual love and wisdom. In one of the most moving conclusions in modern literature, she reveals the unifying principle which holds archetypal forces—and all of creation— together and gives them purpose and direction. She demonstrates the redemptive power of Christ-like love and reaffirms the benevolent nature of life.

Yet neither the plot, as powerful as it is, nor the parallels to the Tarot, as deftly as they are drawn, give

The Greater Trumps its unique quality. Nor is it Williams' characterizations, which are clearly symbolic—Henry representing the arrogant but well-educated intellect, Nancy representing the intuition, Sybil representing redemptive love, and so on.

No, what sets this novel apart from almost all others is its pace and momentum, which is as strong and as forceful as the blizzard Henry carelessly invokes. Williams carefully weaves together the various elements of his plot, then lets the archetypal power of raw creative force take over and sweep us to the inevitable, perfect conclusion of the book.

In chapter after chapter, he gives us brilliant descriptions of the most fundamental conditions of human existence—madness, love, creativity, chaos, self-control, the feminine aspect of life, the masculine force of life, conflict, and the power to triumph over all odds.

In other books, these descriptions would be ponderous, difficult to wade through, but in *The Greater Trumps*, they are the heart of the book. They are filled with the vitality of the story itself and, as the reader finishes each passage, he is tempted to go back and read it again, just to savor it, while impelled to continue reading, to learn what happens next.

We all need to learn the lessons that Henry, Nancy, Sybil, and the other characters of *The Greater Trumps* learn—the lessons of acting, thinking, and feeling in harmony with the rhythms and designs of divine life (to which the Tarot can be a key), not in opposition to them.

The Greater Trumps is an outstanding novel.

Reincarnation
by Leoline L. Wright

The cycles of rebirth constitute one of the most important principles of life, observable not just in nature, the seasons, and the economy, but also in the appearance of human beings in the earth plane. To fully understand the higher self and its methods of manifestation on earth, it is necessary to comprehend the concept of rebirth, or reincarnation.

Unfortunately, it is hard to find *intelligent* discussions of this subject in print. Reincarnation is a concept that is burdened by glamours and distorted by misconceptions; the vast majority of writings about it are nothing more than fantasies about earlier lifetimes or groundless speculations about the meaning of rebirth.

As a result, Leoline L. Wright's small book, *Reincarnation*, stands out as a refreshing exception to the general rule. Written as part of a series of Theosophical manuals on esoteric principles, it is a clear, concise explanation of the principles of rebirth, what it is that reincarnates, why we do not remember past lives, and how the law of rebirth operates.

To quote the text, "The innermost Self of man is a deathless Being, a god, which reclothes itself from age to age in new bodies, that it may undergo all possible experiences in the Universe to which it belongs, and so reach its own most complete growth and self-expression. Rebirth is the pathway of evolution."

As a basic statement of the underlying wisdom of the concept of reincarnation, this book is a unique contribution to human understanding. It is highly recommended.

The Screwtape Letters
by C.S. Lewis

Screwtape is an accomplished devil, an expert at tempting humans and causing them to fall from grace. Wormwood is his nephew—a "junior tempter"—whom Screwtape has taken under his wing, to educate in the fine art of seduction. The result is a series of letters from Screwtape to Wormwood which deserves to be considered a modern masterpiece of both satire and human behavior.

For even though the protagonists of this story are demons, the real subjects are humans trying to come to terms with who they are—one human being in particular, who has been assigned to Wormwood as his "client."

Letter after letter, Screwtape instructs Wormwood in the weaknesses of human nature—self-deception, hypocrisy, pettiness, and selfishness. He exhorts Wormwood to keep his client diverted from a real understanding of "the Enemy"—which is, of course, God—and suggests all manner of ways to do so. In the process, Lewis neatly uses the cutting edge of humor to slice through popular beliefs about attitude and emotion and demonstrate the subtle, thoughtless ways we tempt ourselves—and succumb.

The Screwtape Letters is witty and delightful, a tongue-in-cheek dramatization of the struggle between darkness and light. And even though the author plays humorously off the idea of a devil, it becomes clear that our real struggle is not with some laughable demon, but with the seeds of ignorance and selfishness within our own character.

The Real World of Fairies

by Dora van Gelder

Confined by our senses to the physical world, as most of us are, there is much about the inner dimensions of life which escapes our observation and understanding. And yet, our confinement is mostly voluntary. There are many ways out of it.

One of the most delightful is to spend an afternoon or evening reading *The Real World of Fairies*, a book as charming as the creatures it describes. Dora van Gelder is a gifted clairvoyant who has had a strong rapport with the fairy kingdom since her childhood in Java. Through her personal observations and experiences, we are led into an inner dimension which is everywhere around us, but unknown to the vast majority of humans.

Fairies are creatures of light and motion, a part of the angelic kingdom. They work directly with the forces of nature—fire, earth, air, and water—in supporting and tending the development of life in this marvelous garden, Earth.

In this book, Miss van Gelder describes the various kinds of fairies and their levels of evolution, but she does much more as well. She captures the spirit of beauty and joy which is the basic characteristic of this kingdom of life, and shares it with us. Reading this book, it is possible to learn a great deal about the abstract nature of the inner planes, the way in which light ensouls itself in form, and the intelligence and order of universal law—and yet be entertained and lifted up in spirit all the while.

After We Die, What Then?
by George W. Meek

Few subjects are more important—and more commonly ignored—than just what happens to us following death. Theology has tried to answer the question, but has done little but stir up fear and guilt. Science has also tried to guide us, but has done even worse, succeeding only in planting seeds of doubt.

George W. Meek is an engineer who has led the effort to discover just exactly what does happen after we die. Meek first collected his findings in a book published eight years ago. But he did not stop his research—or his discoveries. So, a new and freshly revised edition was in order.

After We Die, What Then? is possibly the most comprehensive book on the nature of life after death in print today. The book is divided into four parts. In the first, Meek presents an overview of the subject and why it is reasonable to expect life to continue. In the second, he examines the plentiful evidence for survival, from spirit photographs and mediumistic records to near-death memories. This section is followed by a chapter in which Meek answers 50 of the common questions about death.

While some of this material has been updated, the bulk of Meek's new material in this edition is presented in the final section, in which he reports on successful experiments to speak with spirits by radio-like electronic devices.

This book establishes the continuity of life as *fact*, not speculation.

Practical Mysticism
by Evelyn Underhill

"The spiritual life is not a special career, involving abstraction from the world of things. It is a part of every man's life; and until he has realised it he is not a complete human being, has not entered into possession of all his powers. It is therefore the function of a practical mysticism to increase, not diminish, the total efficiency, the wisdom and steadfastness, of those who try to practise it."

With these few words, Evelyn Underhill sets the tone for the whole of *Practical Mysticism,* one of the most lucid and helpful explanations of the art of mysticism ever written. Unlike most authors on the subject, Miss Underhill knows exactly what the mystical state is: the art of union with reality. She therefore does not waste any time gushing emotionally about all the wonders of the abstract life, as so many nouveau mystics do; step by step, she shows us what we must do in order to identify with and unite with reality. And at every step, she makes the extra effort to show how mysticism enriches our daily life in practical ways.

Miss Underhill is especially brilliant in her description of contemplation. For far too many people, contemplation is a lazy, reflective state of adoration or devotion. Not so, Miss Underhill explains; true mystical contemplation requires us to *stretch* beyond our personal capacity and, by an act of will, radiate our adoration or devotion into the whole of creation, transforming it even as we transform ourselves.

Practical Mysticism is a classic in its field. This completely new edition makes it available once again.

The Nine Billion
Names of God
by Arthur C. Clarke

Arthur C. Clarke's great knack as a writer of science fiction and fantasy is his ability to weave what he calls the "Wide View" of life into entertaining stories. Clarke has a firm understanding of how the evolutionary impulse of life challenges, pushes, cajoles, and bullies us humans to grow, in spite of ourselves, and sooner or later, this theme pops up in almost everything he writes.

This is certainly the case in *The Nine Billion Names of God*, a collection of Clarke's 25 favorite short stories among the more than 100 that he has written. From the title story, which flirts deliciously with the creative power of the Word, to the startling, rudely awakening finale of "The Star," these stories expand the scope of our own thinking, about ourselves and about life in general. In its own way, each story challenges preconceived notions and cultural prejudices which tend to keep us from discovering the wider meanings and implications of life.

Yet each story is fresh and original, not just another bucket drawn from the same well. Clarke has amazing dexterity, making us believe he is a mystery writer in "Trouble with Time," the story of an inept art thief on Mars; a humorist in "The Reluctant Orchid," in which the purpose of nurturing love is forgotten, then recovered; and a prophet in "The Sentinel," which became the basis for the film *2001: A Space Odyssey.*

These stories are real gems, the work of a master of science fiction.

Atlas Shrugged
by Ayn Rand

First published in 1957, this great novel by Ayn Rand is still relevant today, as it clearly highlights the basic themes of the Spirit of America and the triumph of the creative individual over the parasitic forces of inertia.

Atlas Shrugged is set in a society which has gone sour through its surrender to elements that champion mediocrity, decry elitism, fear excellence, and are committed to a program of economic cannibalism which slowly destroys the productive elements of society in order to support the tyranny of the masses.

Its heroes are a small group of people who still possess the creative spirit of initiative and self-sufficiency on which America was founded, and cherish the freedoms which make the independence of the individual possible. As the destruction of the fabric of society proceeds, these productive individuals are accused of selfishness, greed, and social irresponsibility. Actually, their only crimes are good sense and an enlightened work ethic.

Finally, they decide they are no longer willing to carry on their backs the hoards of welfare consumers. So they retreat to a secret valley and begin a new society, which fosters genius, initiative, self-sufficiency, and enlightened cooperation.

Atlas, of course, is the Greek Titan who carries the world on his shoulders. He is symbolic of the creative and productive elements of society, which truly support the world. In this great novel, the Atlas finally shrugs off his parasitic burden and achieves freedom.

Esoteric Christianity
by Annie Besant

There are two sides to every major religion—the familiar teachings and creeds the average person associates with the religion, and the inner or esoteric teachings which are the religion's link to the Ancient Wisdom. The familiar teachings of a religion are easily found—in its dogma, its scripture, the life story of its founder, and the writings of its saints or great teachers. The esoteric tradition is usually not so easily found. It is the record of what the visionaries of the religion, from the founder to the present day, have discovered about spirit. Often, it is not even known to most of the religion's priests, having been preserved only in the writings of mystics or passed on orally.

The esoteric side of Christianity certainly fits this pattern. It flourished for the first several centuries after Christ and made a rich contribution to early Christian thought. Its primary guardians at that time were the early Gnostics. But as time passed, dissension within the ranks of the Gnostics betrayed their rich treasure, and political pressures within the Church of Rome forced it underground.

Nevertheless, the inner side of Christianity has survived, carried on by the inspired mystics, saints, and occultists of every century. Indeed, no matter how hard the official church may try to purge these teachings, they will always survive, because they are nothing less than the actual roots of Christianity in the infinite love and wisdom of God. Any enlightened person who studies Christianity "rediscovers" its esoteric side and brings it to our attention again. The flame of truth never dies, even though its outer light may be obscured from time to time.

Annie Besant is clearly one who is attuned to the rich esoteric tradition of Christianity. Her book, *Esoteric Christianity*, is a remarkable exploration of early Christian teachings, how they have been preserved throughout the ages, and their r̲e̲l̲e̲v̲a̲n̲ce to our lives and spiritual growth today.

Mrs. Besant was an early T̲ [...] followed H.P. Blavatsky as preside̲[nt of the The]̲ophical Society and collaborated [with C.W. Lea]dbeater on a number of books—as we̲[ll as writin]g a good many books on her own. *Esoteric C̲[hristi]anity* is one of the best, remaining, even after all these years, a much-needed supplement to the historical record of Christianity. Her search through the surviving writings of early Christian scholars and Gnostics reveals that their insights into the true message of the Christ were both brilliant and pertinent to daily life. She gives us an invaluable glimpse into the practice of Christianity before it became deadened by dogma and arthritic with tradition.

In the early days of Christianity, the central role of intuition to the life of spirit was understood and accepted. The spiritual gifts Paul described were more common and prized. The fact of reincarnation was accepted and a knowledge of the inner planes was considered important to the conduct of a spiritual life on earth. The role of initiation in spiritual growth was respected. Angels were not something that showed up once at the birth of Christ and then no more—the value of invoking these forces was appreciated.

Mrs. Besant begins with a brief examination of how

this esoteric tradition began, what it taught, and how it was "lost." She then turns her attention to a thorough exploration of what she deems the primary themes of esoteric Christianity, relating the story of the historical Christ with the inner teachings of the mythic and mystic Christ, probing the inner meaning of atonement, resurrection, ascension, and the trinity, and concluding with an evaluation of the esoteric value of prayer, forgiveness of sins, the major sacraments, and Christian revelation.

Esoteric Christianity is a major book. The mere fact it could be written is proof the wisdom of God never dies. No matter how many books are burned, or how much political intrigue sabotages religious teachings, nor how many Inquisitions are conducted, the true spirit of religion cannot be surpressed. It will be carried on, and is always available to true esoteric students.

It is also an *exciting* book to read, at least for anyone interested in the inner life of Christianity. Where familiar teachings and dogma fall short, never quite satisfying the enlightened quest for understanding, Mrs. Besant's story of the early teachings clarifies much of what has been obscure and incomplete. It is highly recommended.

Waldo & Magic, Inc.
by Robert Heinlein

Waldo & Magic, Inc. is a double treat, in that it is really two novellas in a single book, both vintage Heinlein and brimming with esoteric significance.

Waldo is the story of a great genius who lives in the isolation of outer space, apart from mankind, which he holds in contempt. But humanity is faced with an energy crisis strangely paralleling a personal affliction Waldo has had since birth—myasthenia gravis.

Waldo has no choice but to return to earth, where he not only unlocks the secret of unlimited energy but also discovers his own tie with humanity, thereby curing himself. The accuracy with which Heinlein portrays the nature of energy is amazing. Few novels are more brilliantly conceived and executed than this one—or more satisfying to read.

Magic, Inc. is a different kind of tale—a major confrontation between the forces of white magic and black magic for control of the government—and through it, the practice of all magic. The confrontation leads the heroes of the story into the "Half World" for the final showdown—in which, of course, light does triumph over darkness.

The action in the "Half World" is a remarkable revelation of the way things actually occur in some dimensions of the astral plane, and what it requires to interact with it safely. As with all Heinlein stories, there is a serious message behind all of the great, good fun and excitement of the actual story.

The two novellas of *Waldo & Magic, Inc.* represent esoteric fiction at its best.

The Seven Human Temperaments
by Geoffrey Hodson

One of the most fascinating new teachings to emerge in the last 100 years has been the concept of the seven rays—that there are seven divine energies which are the creative builders of all of life. Out of these seven rays, in an almost infinite number of combinations, everything that is has been created. An understanding of these rays, therefore, and how they act at the inner levels of life to produce changes and growth at the outer levels, provides enormous insight into our understanding of just about every facet of life.

The workings of the rays, however, is a complex subject; many contemporary authors have made a muddle of them, misconstruing their true esoteric meaning. As fascinating as the subject is, therefore, we should take care to study it with discernment, and not succumb to fanciful but inaccurate information.

Beyond any doubt, the best introduction to the rays currently in print is *The Seven Human Temperaments* by Geoffrey Hodson. Hodson, an outstanding clairvoyant, limits his treatment of the rays to their influence on humanity, yet nonetheless presents a very readable discussion of each ray, its ideal, and some of the ways people behave under its influence. He also provides a very interesting chart which makes it easy to study similarities and differences among the rays.

Far more work will be done on the importance of the rays in the future. But for a good, solid foundation in the subject, *The Seven Human Temperaments* is the place to begin.

EDGAR CAYCE'S STORY OF ATTITUDES & EMOTIONS
by Jeffrey Furst

Edgar Cayce is certainly the best-known psychic America has yet produced, and his work is a veritable treasure of esoteric insights. Over a span of 40 years he gave some 15,000 psychic readings, all of which have been carefully preserved.

One of the areas in which the Cayce readings are the most profound is in their commentary on the roots of our emotional problems, their relation to physical illness, and the power we have to redirect and enlighten our attitudes and emotions.

Author Jeffrey Furst has researched key passages in the Cayce readings dealing with emotional problems and their cures, drawn them together, and added commentary of his own to tie it all together.

The result is *Edgar Cayce's Story of Attitudes and Emotions*, a thoroughly readable and very helpful examination of emotions, ethics, feelings, and morality. It pulls no punches in describing the true effect of negative emotions such as fear, anger, envy, and depression on ourselves and others, or in describing how gossip, criticism, and selfishness damage our subtle bodies—our psychological mechanism.

At the same time, it makes clear the value of cultivating wholesome emotions such as goodwill, tolerance, cheerfulness, calmness, and compassion—and our capacity to harmonize extremes.

We all have much to learn about our use of the emotions. *Edgar Cayce's Story of Attitudes and Emotions* makes an excellent workbook for personal growth.

The Tao of Power
by R.L. Wing

Lao Tzu's *Tao Te Ching* is one of the great books of the world, second only in number of translations and printings to the Bible. Yet finding an *inspired* translation suitable to the modern West has been difficult. It is therefore with great enthusiasm that we greet the publication of R.L. Wing's new translation of this classic text, *The Tao of Power*.

The Chinese word "tao," as Wing explains, is a word Lao Tzu coined to represent the way the universe works. The word "te" signifies the power or natural force within any element of life. The purpose of the *Tao*, therefore, is to teach us the way we can harness the natural force or power of a situation to serve the divine plan—in our own life, a business, a group, or a nation. It is not a guide to attaining power, but rather a text on what to do with the power which lies latent in all conditions of life—the power of opportunity.

Lao Tzu does this through 81 verses, written, so the legend goes, just before his retirement from an active political life during one of the most competitive, warring dynasties of China.

Wing, who established his reputation with *The I Ching Workbook*, expands it with this new work. He translates each of the 81 verses clearly, adds his own commentary, and frequently provides an illustration of some kind as a further comment.

In addition, he has written several preliminary chapters which illumine the meaning of the Tao for us—and give us a way to use it as a new mantic device.

Great Lion of God
by Taylor Caldwell

"Many novels and books about St. Paul have told in marvelous detail what he *did* and accomplished in his life and missionary journeys. I am concerned with what he *was*, a man like ourselves with our own despairs, doubts, anxieties and angers and intolerances, and 'lusts of the flesh.' Many books have been concerned with the Apostle. I am concerned with the man, the human being, as well as the dauntless saint."

So writes Taylor Caldwell in the introduction to her historical novel, *Great Lion of God*, a fictionalized account of the life of St. Paul. What follows the introduction is a masterful fulfillment of her goal—a tremendous story with universal appeal.

It is really the story of struggle. Paul was born into a wealthy Jewish family and educated as a Pharisee. To pursue a closer relationship with God, and service to the Christ, he cut himself off from the support of his family, his friends, his wealth, and his religion. He estranged himself from the life of earth to know the life of heaven, and reveal it to others.

And yet, none of these sacrifices came easily. Paul was a highly sensitive person, torn between the pairs of opposites that every spiritual aspirant must face. He knew well his human weaknesses—but he valued even more the love of God.

Taylor Caldwell is brilliant at getting inside the thoughts and feelings, the values and motivations of her characters. *Great Lion of God* is not just a story of Paul; it is the story of every human being who struggles to become a servant of God.

Life as Carola
by Joan Grant

Carola is the illegitimate daughter of one of the most powerful noblemen in Italy. Yet she and her mother are forced to leave the family castle and wander penniless. They join a band of strolling actors, crisscrossing northern Italy in search of the right opportunity to establish themselves. But opportunity always seems to elude them. Eventually, they break up and Carola enters a convent as a novice.

By this time, she is 18 and has developed many psychic abilities. But the other sisters in the convent do not understand the nature of Carola's gifts. She is accused of witchcraft and forced to undergo torture, until she manages to escape and finds refuge at last.

Like the other novels of Joan Grant, *Life as Carola* is a retelling of a previous life of the author. It is a more difficult life than the one led in *Winged Pharaoh*, but on the whole, it is even more spell-binding.

On one level, *Life as Carola* is a fascinating glimpse into life in Italy just before the advent of the Renaissance. Through Carola's eyes, we see the beginnings of modern theater, the tremendous extremes between the life of nobility and the common man, and even the awakening of Europe to the existence of the Americas.

Yet the real power of this book is its personal account of a very intimate story—the growth and development of the inner character of a young woman, and her capacity to triumph in even the most adverse situations. This is a book filled with all the best qualities of human nature.

Life as Carola is must reading.

The Space Trilogy
by C.S. Lewis

C.S. Lewis was an intense student of the nature of God and divine involvement in the affairs of mankind. As a professor at Cambridge University, he wrote many philosophical pieces on Christian ethics. But fortunately for us, he did not limit himself to scholarly writing. He also wrote several masterpieces of fiction, including *The Space Trilogy*.

This collection of novels is once again dramatic proof that fiction is often the best vehicle for treating the nature of good and evil, because the struggle between nobility and baseness is a vintage human struggle. In the hands of a master storyteller, it inevitably forms the basis of a gripping tale, as well as providing us with the opportunity to rehearse vicariously for our own struggles with evil.

The action begins in *Out of the Silent Planet*. Lewis's hero, Professor Ransom, is kidnapped by mad scientists Devine and Weston and taken to another planet. Once there, Ransom escapes and discovers that the focal point of civilized life on this planet is the presence of God. *Eldila*, which are something like angels, commonly appear to the human beings inhabiting the planet, speaking as agents of God.

In fact, the attitude of these people toward God differs remarkably from the attitudes prevailing on earth, which is known as "the silent planet" because God is unable to communicate directly to the unheeding earthlings. Ransom seizes the opportunity of being on this planet to explore the nature of God, first in discussions with the local inhabitants and then directly through his own experiences. In this way, Lewis adroitly weaves in his perspectives on the unity of life and the order of divine intelligence.

Knowing the reality and force of divine law, the people of this planet willingly cooperate with it. Knowing the purpose of God, they work to fulfill it. Knowing the power and benevolence of God, they trust their Creator fully.

Devine and Weston, representing the worst of ignorant materialism and godlessness in human society, stand in stark contrast. At the end of the novel, they are brought before the spiritual intelligence in charge of the planet. Confronting this great intelligence, the absurdity and pettiness of their evil nature is revealed.

In *Perelandra*, Ransom journeys to the planet of that name, where Weston is once more trying to find his fortune illicitly. The nature of Perelandra is unique. It is a new planet where death does not occur and the entire human race is a *single* Lady-Mother. Weston is possessed by an earth devil who cunningly employs all the propaganda, lies, and distortions he has learned on earth in an attempt to seduce the Eve-like Lady-Mother.

The dialogues between this devil and the Lady-Mother are quite possibly the finest in print on the nature of temptation and the rationalizations we use for defying the will of God. Some of the arguments the devil uses—the need to be self-sufficient, independent, and strong in order to overcome exploitation—strike exceedingly close to home in modern society.

In the final battle, Ransom almost exhausts his strength and sanity, and prays to God for deliverance. But in the end, he realizes that *he is the miracle* he prayed for—that God does work, but *through him*. This enables him to defeat the devil and discover that he has served the human race of this planet as Christ served the people on earth in His time. This struggle helps us appreciate that the nature of evil is often very subtle—and even attractive. In the hands of deceitful people, reason and logic can become tools of evil.

The final book of the trilogy, *That Hideous Strength*, takes place in modern England. A small group of university professors and scientists, embodying the principles of scientific pragmatism and logical positivism, set out to take over a university town, aided by the "hideous strength" of evil intelligences. The ultimate goal, of course, is to take over all of society, and the parallel with Nazi Germany is unmistakable. The arrogance and materialism of the group is striking as it strives to seize control by manipulating the press, intimidating the townspeople, and exploiting crises to gain acceptance of their tyrannical rule.

A small cadre of people led by Professor Ransom are aware of the evil at hand. With the help of a young clairvoyant woman, they struggle to contain and defeat the fascist forces. But their own resources are not enough, so they summon the presence of Merlin, the ancient magician of King Arthur's court, to help them in the fray. In this way, they are able to defeat the evil of the present day with magic from ancient times.

The Space Trilogy deserves to be acclaimed as a masterpiece of metaphysical fiction.

Life Everlasting
by Murdo MacDonald-Bayne

The words of a truly inspired teacher are a rare treasure. One such teacher was Murdo MacDonald-Bayne, a Scotsman who carried the teachings of the Masters throughout the world just a few short decades ago. The inspiration and insight of MacDonald-Bayne have been available for some time now in several books, most notably *Divine Healing of Mind and Body*. Recently, however, a new book has been added to those already published—*Life Everlasting*.

Life Everlasting is a collection of 26 lectures delivered by MacDonald-Bayne in the late forties to his students in South Africa. But it is more than just a collection of talks on the nature of spirit. *Life Everlasting* is a powerful description of the reality of Life.

"If you are not in love with Life," he writes, "Life will make you unhappy and force you to be in love with it, by sorrow, by pain. It will lead you into deep waters so that you will have to struggle. When you understand Life, struggling will cease and you will love Life as Life loves you."

In such simple, lucid language, MacDonald-Bayne leads us, step by step, into a greater and more profound realization of just what life is and our relationship with it. He writes with the authority of one who has learned from personal experience as well as from teachers.

In the first lecture, he provides a brief sketch of his own personal odyssey. In the late 1930's, when he was about 50 years old, he was led by an inner urging to travel to the monastery of a Tibetan master, who helped him refine his already considerable spiritual talents. When this advanced training was complete, he began his mission, which took him around the world lecturing, healing, and establishing centers of light.

As in the case of the lectures in *Divine Healing of Mind and Body*, MacDonald-Bayne's students report that he was frequently overshadowed by a powerful, spiritual presence while delivering the lectures collected in *Life Everlasting*. This presence was seen at times by some of the students as a visible form, but was generally felt by all in attendance as a commanding force of great benevolent wisdom.

But the value of this book lies not in its inspired origin but in its *substance*. Readers who are just beginning to acquaint themselves with esoteric literature will delight in the clarity of the ideas presented, while those who are thoroughly familiar with esoteric concepts will be challenged by the penetrating truth with which MacDonald-Bayne presents his ideas.

"The real work of humanity," he explains, "is to recognize and free the Divine Spirit in man, to recognize that all power comes from within, that no one has any more power than another." In chapter after chapter, he brilliantly develops this theme, demonstrating how we trap ourselves in erroneous beliefs, wrongly identify with our own mental creations and sensations, and blind ourselves in illusions of our own making.

"What frees us from all our limitation," he continues, "is to recognize our unity with the Infinite Universal Life. The Universal Life is impersonal and makes no exception in favor of any individual. The Universal Life does not act from anger, jealousy, or wrath. Neither can it be flattered, cajoled, or moved by sympathy or petition. It works through cooperation and he who understands this appears to be favored because he has found the source of all wealth, health, and power."

MacDonald-Bayne explores at length the ways in which we generate misery and disease in our lives through the beliefs and illusions we hold *about* life. Time and again he stresses that concepts *about* life are no substitute for direct awareness of life and disciplining our attitudes, thoughts, and behavior so that we create in our mind and self-expression conditions and concepts that reflect the divine instead of our personal illusions.

In fact, he is quite insistent about the danger of failing to go beyond the mere intellectual possession of truth concepts. The truth that sets us free and reveals the life of spirit is something to identify with—something to know by being it and expressing it in our thoughts and acts. All too many travelers on the spiritual path fail to learn this vital lesson and remain imprisoned by their own ideas and beliefs.

He therefore encourages us not to evaluate our progress by what we believe or know, but by *who we are*. He challenges us us to examine the content of our moods, ideas, habits, and actions and discard those which clash with the reality of life. In this way, we can identify with spiritual *fact*, and leave the "cage" of our illusions behind.

Life Everlasting is a marvelous book. Its wisdom can indeed lead us to life everlasting—if we heed it.

The Fullness of Human Experience
by Dane Rudhyar

Dane Rudhyar, who died in 1985 at the age of 90, was one of the clearest thinkers and writers of our age. We have long wanted to feature one of his books, yet many of the most readily available are highly specialized. It is therefore with pleasure that we recommend his final book, *The Fullness of Human Experience*.

This new book is a fitting climax to Rudhyar's extensive body of writings, as it takes many of the essential themes he dealt with throughout his life and focuses them in one ultimate investigation—an investigation into the meaning and purpose of human life and individuality, from which he draws conclusions as to what values, practices, and pursuits lead to the "fullness" of human activity.

Rudhyar begins by restating his basic concept of wholeness and the experience of periodic change, showing how the individual fits into the larger whole, draws his meaning from it, and must be interpreted within a holistic context. He goes on to point out that certain rhythms of change govern both the whole and the individual, generating opportunity, problems, challenges, crises, and growth.

Somewhere on the road between fatalistic superstition and existential nonsense, the human mind begins to sense and become aware of these rhythms and cooperate with them. As this occurs, his or her true individuality grows.

The Fullness of Human Experience is the crowning achievement of a mature mind.

Moon Magic
by Dion Fortune

"The moon is riding high and clear,
O Lovely one, draw near, draw near;
To lonely men on lonely ways
Come down in dream of silver haze.
Persephone, Persephone,
All in the end shall come to thee."

The sequel to *The Sea Priestess*, in which Dion Fortune introduced the character of Vivien Le Fay Morgan or Lilith Le Fay, *Moon Magic* is a haunting, powerful novel, one of a kind. For it is written through the persona of Lilith herself, who claims to be a priestess of the goddess Isis—the divine feminine principle.

As such, this novel boldly explores the archetypal forces of manhood, womanhood, and sexuality, and unveils the inner levels of magic which work through them in the great drama of creativity. *Moon Magic* does not hesitate to shake worn-out customs and rituals until they are exposed, but it does a great deal more than shock. It is a finely tuned novel, which leads us step by step to a truer awareness of what is involved in establishing a profound intuitive rapport with the inner forces and dimensions of life.

The symbol of the moon, of course, is an ancient one for the feminine principle and its unique capacity to unleash the full potency of the masculine principle and produce union—between two lovers, the personality and the soul, and humanity and the divine.

In the final analysis, *Moon Magic* is a mystery novel—a novel which explores the mystery of who we are in a thoroughly captivating way.

Life Force
by Colin Wilson

The men and women that the crew of the spaceship *Hermes* found on a distressed craft certainly appeared dead. But they did not exactly seem human—they were almost too perfect for that—so the crew brought them back to earth for tests and evaluations. All went well, until a reporter wormed his way into the top secret laboratory to get the story of the century. In seconds, he was dead—his life force sucked out of him by one of the aliens, who was now suddenly alive.

So begins the story of *Life Force* (originally titled *The Space Vampires*) a marvelous novel by Colin Wilson that is the perfect companion to his earlier classic, *The Mind Parasites*. A thrilling adventure story, *Life Force* is also much more—a brilliant study of the exchange of life energy among humans, the pathologies of psychic vampirism, the roots of criminal insanity, and the inner dimensions of sexuality.

It ends with one of the most finely-etched descriptions of healing ever put on paper, as the space vampires are drawn back into a realization that all life emanates from a central source of light, and no one need steal from anyone else.

In between is vintage Colin Wilson, a story which is as informative as it is exciting. There is tremendous insight in this book into the nature of the subconscious and unconscious forces at work in the mind—and human relationships. Wilson sharply delineates the difference between *receiving* and *taking* energy.

Life Force is a landmark work of fiction. It is highly recommended.

The Four Lords of the Diamond
by Jack L. Chalker

Jack Chalker is a writer with an extraordinary talent for creating strange worlds which powerfully dramatize cosmic ideas and principles. He did it in his five-novel series, *Saga of the Well World*, and he does it again in his four-novel set, *The Four Lords of the Diamond*.

The four novels are set in the Warden Diamond—four planets that serve as a penal colony for the most intelligent criminal minds in a vast confederacy of planets. These four worlds are the untouchables of space, because once anyone lands on them, a strange microscopic life form invades his system. If he then leaves the Diamond, he dies.

The Warden organism is a central part of the mystery of these four stories. It permeates all substance and life, acting as a unifying life force throughout the Diamond. As a group of new arrivals to the Warden are told: "Every single thing you see—not just the grass and trees, but everything: rocks, the very dirt under your feet—is alive, all cells of a single organism, each of which has its own Warden organism inside it in the same symbiotic relationship it is establishing in your bodies....Somehow, nobody knows how, all Warden organisms are linked together. You might think of them as single independent cells of a great creature."

Within the body of this great creature, the drama of these four novels unfolds. In fact, the untouchable nature of the Diamond, long a blessing to the free worlds of the Confederacy, has now become a major problem. The criminal overlords of these four planets have entered into a secret partnership with powerful alien beings, who intend to use the Diamond as a staging area to invade all the planets in the Confederacy.

But the Confederacy cannot just invade the Diamond and eliminate the problem, because whoever would be sent could never return. So a unique solution is hit upon: four of the worst criminals left in the Confederacy are captured and their minds are washed clean. They are sent to the Diamond, one to each planet, to search out the overlord of that world, assassinate him, take his place, and find out about the aliens and their plans. These agents are controlled mentally by an Agent With No Name who stays safely outside.

Each book is the adventure of one of these agents. In the first, *Lilith: A Snake in the Grass*, the agent learns that the Warden organism is not just a powerful force which keeps people from leaving the Diamond; it can also be tapped to develop useful skills and talents. In order to fulfill his mission, the agent learns to use etheric sight and manipulate the life force of matter, both to build and destroy physical forms.

In the second book, *Cerberus: A Wolf in the Fold*, the Warden organism is tapped to transfer the mind into other bodies, enabling everyone to experience what it means to be male and female. As a result, people learn to recognize each other by their consciousness, not their bodies. This book contains some of the most brilliant discussion of the subtle forms and dynamics of consciousness to be found anywhere in print.

In *Charon: A Dragon at the Gate*, the Warden organism has a different impact: it permits the people of

Charon to become great magicians. The agent sent to replace the overlord must therefore learn to deal with this magic, leading to a tremendous struggle—and the discovery that the ability to communicate with the Warden organism is the ultimate weapon of magic.

The planet of the fourth novel, *Medusa: A Tiger by the Tail*, is the harshest of all, a cold and desolate place. But the agent does manage to encounter the aliens, forcing him to deal with mystical forces, alien bodies, and mortal danger simultaneously. In the process, he discovers that the aliens are something quite different than expected. The showdown which has been building for four novels concludes with a wonderful twist—the emergence of a new and powerful intelligence. The whole "alien invasion" had been planned by the Warden organism for the good of evolutionary development. The parallel with the idea of a planetary Logos and Hierarchy guiding the emerging civilization of earth is unmistakable.

The Four Lords of the Diamond is a marvelous saga—the brilliant work of an inspired author.

Return to Elysium
by Joan Grant

Lucina is a Greek girl who grows up in an Utopian enclave, Elysium. As she matures, her natural psychic talents unfold—putting her at odds with Aesculapius, the philosopher and doctor who founded Elysium and is Lucina's guardian.

At first, Aesculapius feigns a scientific interest in Lucina's talents, and suggests that they work together to prove or disprove them. He sets up an experiment designed to trick Lucina, but she uncovers the ruse and passes the test. Aesculapius, unable to accept the facts, reneges on his promise to help Lucina.

Unable to grow further in Elysium, Lucina and two friends sail to Rome, which is just emerging as an empire. There she becomes a priestess in a Delphic temple, dispensing wisdom and healing to any who come. Her reputation grows quickly, but without solid training, success becomes more of a curse than a blessing. At the height of her career, she abandons it all to run away with her lover, a Roman senator.

Return to Elysium is a delightful book to read, filled with insights into human nature. It portrays the conflict between science and intuition—and also provides us with a profound description of the power of self-deception, buttressed by solely intellectual assumptions, to prevent us from understanding ourself and our destiny.

One of seven far memory novels by Joan Grant, *Return to Elysium* also features one of the most intriguing endings in all of modern literature.

This is first-rate esoteric fiction.

Visible Light
by C.J. Cherryh

"A story is a moment of profound examination of things in greater reality and sharper focus than we usually see them." With this statement, C.J. Cherryh introduces the short stories in *Visible Light*, all of which are written with the brilliance and imagination of a master story teller who takes us *beyond* ordinary perspectives, into the inner side of life.

In "Casandra," for instance, we are taken inside the personality of a clairvoyant woman who must live with a continual and maddening awareness of the disastrous future of those about her. It reminds us that too much attention given to our future, good or bad, can so frustrate us that we spoil our current opportunities.

"Threads of Time" is a tale about the time police, who work to stop those who would tamper with the present by changing the past. The story vividly teaches us how easily opportunities are lost—and difficulties created.

The story "Companions" concerns a marooned spaceman and his robot aide. In it, we learn about the many facets of the human mind, as the hero confronts himself in his loneliness. In the process, we learn how our concrete thinking can imprison and destroy our spiritual dimensions.

Cherryh says we tend to systematize what we see and then see what we want, and thereby end up making fools of ourselves. To stop this tendency, we must learn to penetrate our assumptions and habits and see things as they are. The stories in *Visible Light* are all mind stretchers guaranteed to make us more thoughtful and perceptive.

Magic Kingdom for Sale
by Terry Brooks

In an attempt to escape a successful but boring life as an attorney, Ben Holiday buys Landover, a magic kingdom, for one million dollars. To his dismay, he gets what he paid for—and a whole lot more.

The kingdom is in ruin. The Barons refuse to recognize a king, and demons, a dragon, and an evil witch threaten the country. His entourage is small: an incompetent magician, a talking dog, and a tree. Even the Paladin, champion of the kings, seems to be just a myth.

Holiday, of course, proves to be a worthy king, and overcomes all these obstacles. Author Terry Brooks keeps the action moving breathlessly—so well, in fact, we might miss the story's subtleties.

In point of fact, the story is a marvelous allegory of the spiritual path. The real magic kingdom is the life of consciousness; we all have one within us, but mostly ignore it. Once we discover we have this inner kingdom, we enter the spiritual path. But like Holiday, we find it is not all fun and games. There are inner realities (the reluctant barons) who will not obey us. And there are emotional conditions (the river folk and fairies) which seem even more illogical and unruly.

At the end, almost exhausted, Holiday must face almost certain defeat—the chief demon (the dweller on the threshold). This proves too much, until the Paladin (the soul) comes to his rescue, endowing him with superhuman gifts. In this portrait of the third initiation, the story ends.

The real magic kingdom is within us. Terry Brook's fine book helps us find it.

The Light Within Us
by Carl Japikse

There are many people who are sincerely devoted to growing spiritually and becoming more attuned to their higher selves, yet do not make much progress. They try this method and that technique, but exhaust themselves in a series of false starts. They have enough devotion. What they lack is *understanding*—knowledge of how to tread the spiritual path.

The Light Within Us provides this special knowledge. It is a step-by-step guide to spiritual growth which is written to help aspirants of all backgrounds understand what spirit is, what it means to grow spiritually, and how to do it. Written by Carl Japikse, it is a lucid and easy-to-grasp presentation of the timeless knowledge of who we are and why we are here.

The instructions which form the core of the text are a modern, updated translation of an ancient text on raja yoga written thousands of years ago by a teacher named Patanjali. Japikse has taken this basic text, transcribed it into contemporary English, and added his own penetrating insights into spiritual growth.

The result is a profound examination of the spiritual path. The text is split into four parts. The first examines the nature of consciousness. The second describes the process of integration. The third explores creative mastery. The fourth is entitled, "The Light of the World."

The Light Within Us is a guide for all who truly want to grow and discover their heritage of light. It is highly recommended.

The Inner Life
by C.W. Leadbeater

"One of the worst features of modern life is its eager readiness to believe evil—its habit of deliberately seeking out the worst conceivable construction that can be put upon everything. And this attitude is surely at its very worst when adopted toward those who have helped us, to whom we owe thanks for knowledge or inspiration received. Remember the words of the Master: 'Ingratitude is not one of our vices.' It is always a mistake to rush madly into criticism of those who know more than we; it is more seemly to wait and see what the future brings forth. Apply the test of time and the result; 'by their fruits ye shall know them.' Let us make a rule to think the best of every man; let us do our work and leave others free to do theirs."

So writes C.W. Leadbeater on the topic of criticism in *The Inner Life,* one of the greatest books on the nature of the inner planes and spiritual growth ever written.

Leadbeater received his share of criticism during his career. Yet his books have withstood the test of time. If we judge the author by the fruit he bore, C.W. Leadbeater is surely one of the outstanding lights of the new age.

The Inner Life is particularly profound because Leadbeater was one of the greatest clairvoyants of his time. His clairvoyance was not just limited to astral phenomena, as is usually the case, but extended to the mental plane. The depth and clarity of his observations are therefore in a class by themselves.

This is important, because we do not have many reliable guides to the inner life. Some religious and mystical writings do provide us with clues and descriptions but, unfortunately, far too many religious writings end up presenting a very narrow view of life.

Mediums have given us another source of commentary on the nature of the inner life, but in all too many cases these descriptions are unreliable. The great weakness of mediumship (and the fad phenomenon of channeling) is that it is so easily colored by the subconscious expectations of the medium.

As a result, it is common to hear people—even in metaphysics—simply state, when asked about the inner life: "Nobody knows." This uncertainty is then countered by the rigidity of fundamentalism—that we do not need to know, *just believe*.

Well, C.W. Leadbeater *did* know, and *The Inner Life* is a lucid, articulate, and thorough description of what he knew about the spiritual dimensions of life.

The book is a collection of lectures and talks the Bishop delivered to students at the headquarters of the Theosophical Society in Adyar, India, during the summer of 1910. These talks have been edited and arranged by subject into a comprehensive tour of the inner life. The contents include:

- The Great Ones and the way to them.
- Religion.
- The Theosophical attitude.
- The higher planes.
- The Ego and his vehicles.
- The after-death life.
- Astral work.
- The mental body and the power of thought.
- Psychic faculties.
- Devas and nature spirits.

- Reincarnation.
- Karma.

Leadbeater's comments on each of these topics are based on his own direct observation of the way life is, not just physically, but at its inner dimensions as well. In talking about criticism and prejudice, for instance, the Bishop proceeds to state that these conditions are like diseases of the mind. In fact, he becomes quite specific:

"If a prejudice should grow up in the man, thought on that particular subject ceases altogether, and a small eddy forms in which the mental matter runs round and round until it coagulates and becomes a kind of wart....This foul thickened mass blocks all free movement either outward or inward; it prevents him on the one hand from seeing accurately...and on the other from sending out any clear thought.

"These diseased spots in the mental body are unfortunately also centers of infection; the inability to see clearly increases and spreads....Religious prejudice... completely prevents any approach to rational thought with regard to the subject. Unfortunately, a very large number of people have the whole of that part of their mental bodies which should be occupied with religious matters inactive, ossified and covered with warts, so that even the most rudimentary conception of what religion really is remains utterly impossible for them."

This kind of brilliant description of the true nature of the life within us makes *The Inner Life* one of the most valuable books of its kind. It should be part of the library of every serious student.

The Apprentice Adept
by Piers Anthony

Stile has a problem—or an advantage, depending upon one's point of view. He exists in two worlds at the same time. One of the worlds, Proton, is scientific, materialistic, and environmentally ruined; life there can exist only in domed cities. The other world, Phaze, is a natural paradise where magic rules, instead of science.

Proton is governed by a small number of very wealthy citizens, while the bulk of the population, like Stile, are serfs. Phaze is loosely governed by powerful adepts of magic, whom most of the population fear.

Many of the people in Proton also exist in the magical world of Phaze, although few recognize this fact. In addition to people, Proton has intelligent robots with human-like emotions and self-will. Phaze, by contrast, has golems—magical creatures formed out of wood and animated by the Brown Adept. Even more intriguing is the fact that Proton has horses while Phaze has magical unicorns that are capable of shifting into human shapes and intellects.

Indeed, Phaze is populated by many magical creatures: goblins, dragons, werewolves, vampire bats, demons, harpies, ogres, and trolls. All of these entities have near-human intelligence, and some seem to represent the baser aspects of human nature.

At first, Stile does not realize that he exists in both worlds, but he learns soon enough. For some reason, someone on Proton is trying to kill him. He escapes only because a robot helps him slip into Phaze through the "curtain" that separates the worlds.

Escaping into Phaze does not alleviate Stile's problems, however. On the contrary, he soon discovers that his alternate self on Phaze has already been murdered by sorcery—and he is due to be the next victim.

The three novels in Piers Anthony's marvelous series, *The Apprentice Adept*, chronicle the story of Stile as he shuttles from Proton to Phaze and back again, always one step ahead of his assassin. The story begins in *Split Infinity*, becomes more entangled in *Blue Adept*, and is finally resolved in *Juxtaposition*.

As the story unfolds, Stile realizes that his only hope is to master each of the two worlds. On Proton, this means competing in the Great Games—Olympic-like games in which the single winner is given the status of citizen and immense wealth and privileges. On Phaze, it means Stile must become an adept and master its magical forces.

Working with this premise, Anthony spins a marvelous and exciting allegory of our own existence and spiritual challenges. Like Stile, each of us lives in two worlds— the physical and the astral—simultaneously, even though we usually do not recognize it. The physical is very much like Proton, while the astral is stunningly like Phaze.

Also like Stile, each of us is challenged to become spiritual masters of the worlds we live in. To achieve this, however, we must overcome not only all manner of opposition but also a broad gamut of temptation. In this regard, there is a great deal we can learn from Stile.

At almost every turn, Stile is stymied by the power and corruption of the two worlds. On Proton, it is science and money which bring power to the citizens; on Phaze, it is magic and fear that the adepts use to sustain their power.

Gradually, Stile realizes it would be deadly to succumb to the ever-present temptation to use these "worldly ways." Instead, he commits himself to wage the battle without compromising his integrity—even though his foes cheat at will, and it often seems that Stile will go down to defeat unless he also cheats.

Stile, however, remains loyal to his ethics. While the power they have coveted eventually corrupts his enemies, even greater power comes to Stile, enabling him to triumph.

Our lives intersect the inner worlds more than we suspect. In these stories, demons are conjured by word; in real life, any angry person can summon demonic energies just by the focus of his rage. The spiritual person knows how important it is to control this "magic" with wisdom and ethics.

The Apprentice Adept is a feast of entertainment, rich in insight into the human condition. Reading these novels has a magical way of helping us see our own lives from a more mature view.

The Betty Book
by Stewart Edward White

If one were to draw up a list of the 25 most important classics in the field of spiritual growth and the inner life, *The Betty Book* would probably be somewhere in the top 10. Amid all the current hubbub about "channelling," it is sometimes easy to forget that some of the very best books on the nature of the inner life and our exploration of it were written 50 years ago—or more.

The Betty Book stands in a class by itself. First published in 1937, it chronicles more than 20 years of mediumistic exploration conducted by Stewart White through the mediumship of his wife Betty. What makes *The Betty Book* so outstanding, though, is that it is not just the usual collection of evidential communications with "dead" mothers and aunts. It is a carefully reasoned, lucid exploration of the inner side of our being and what it means to "grow in spirit."

Betty is helped in this work by the "Invisibles," a group of discarnates who take turns speaking through Betty or leading her through an experiment or experience which she then reports back to Stewart. As such, the quality of mediumship and discovery in this book (and subsequent ones written by Stewart) is much higher and more refined than in the usual book on channeling or mediumship.

Beyond that, the insights into human life are both fascinating and compelling. They make sense—and challenge us to rethink our assumptions. *The Betty Book* introduces us to the grandest adventure of all—the discovery of our own inner self.

The Razor's Edge
by W. Somerset Maugham

"The sharp edge of a razor is difficult to pass over; thus the wise say the path to Salvation is hard."

With this quote from the Upanishads as his motto, Somerset Maugham begins his stirring novel of self-discovery and enlightenment, *The Razor's Edge*. It is a novel of a group of friends who repeatedly cross paths in different locales throughout the world, as they sample the pleasures and sorrows of Experience.

The focal point of the story is Larry, who seeks to give his experiences meaning. But it is not just Larry who attempts to walk on the razor's edge—it is actually every character: Elliott, the snob; Isabel, the socialite; Gray, the "regular guy"; Suzanne, the artist's model; and Sophie, lost in wantonness. They continually jab their feet and suffer the consequences.

Overtly, they learn very little from their experiences—except Larry. Larry takes his confusion seriously. He travels to India to find someone who can enlighten him. After many disappointments, he finally locates an ashram. He stays there for two years, until he finally realizes that enlightenment comes from wise living, not withdrawal into solitary contemplation.

So he returns to Paris and reenters the web of relationships spun by his friends. But he is free of the assumptions and limitations that cripple his friends. He moves through life with a grace they observe, but cannot duplicate.

The Razor's Edge is a powerful novel, full of insight into the duality of human reactiveness and what it means to harmonize it.

A Search in Secret India
by Paul Brunton

Paul Brunton was one of the great husbandmen who toiled in the fields of humanity, sowing the seeds of spirituality in the West during the first half of this century, so that we might reap the harvest now that the century is ending. Trained as a journalist, he traveled widely through India and Egypt, learning the spiritual traditions of these great cultures. He then devoted his life to sharing what he had learned in a remarkable series of books.

A Search in Secret India was the first of these books to appear, and it remains today one of the most fascinating and enlightening books available on the Eastern traditions of spiritual growth. It is the highly entertaining report of Brunton's own travels and experiences in seeking out, talking, and studying with some of the most colorful spiritual figures of India fifty years ago—both genuine saints and first-class fakes.

At times, the narrative stretches the Western imagination, because some of the feats described defy our present understanding. But Brunton never overrates these phenomena. He knows that the true power of spirit lies in awareness, not magic, and continually seeks out the true presence of the light within. More often than not, he finds it—and we do, too.

As the *London Times* said, "His work is excellent. It has life, color, movement. Readers will find their interest unflagging from the first page to the last." Indeed, the search leads Brunton to his teacher, and spiritual unfoldment. It has the power to help others in the same way, too.

Masters and Men
by Virginia Hanson

One of the most remarkable phenomena of the early days of Theosophy was the correspondence which occurred between A.P. Sinnet and two of the Masters, Koot Hoomi and Morya.

Sinnet was a journalist who met H.P. Blavatsky soon after her arrival in India, following the publication of *Isis Unveiled.* Impressed by the materialization of messages from the Masters, he asked her to forward a letter of his own to them. To his surprise, an answer materialized in his locked room several days later—and thus the correspondence began.

The actual letters from the Masters to Sinnet are a historical fact, on display in the British Museum. But the letters themselves do not convey the whole story behind this unique correspondence—the story of Madame Blavatsky, Sinnet, H.P. Olcott, and the tumultuous formative years of the Theosophical Socity.

Wanting to retell this story, author Virginia Hanson chose to take the actual facts and documents and assemble them in the form of a narrative. The result is *Masters and Men,* a novel focusing on the interaction between the superphysical masters and the very human men and women who served as their agents.

This is not just a story for those with an interest in the early days of Theosophy. It is a story of importance to all spiritual aspirants, because it reveals how difficult it is to bring new ideas into human awareness—and how important the guidance of our "Elder Brothers" is.

Masters and Men is highly recommended.

Eyes of Horus
by Joan Grant

Ra-ab is the son of the ruler of Oryx, one of the provinces of ancient Egypt. His childhood is a pleasant one, because the Oryx is at peace—and wisely ruled by his father. But such is not the case throughout the rest of Egypt.

The government and religion of this proud nation have been corrupted, taken over almost entirely by dark forces. No longer is Pharaoh a strong, divinely-inspired leader; instead, he rules by fear and imposes unjust taxes. No longer is the temple a sanctuary of truth and light; the true religion has been supplanted by the worship of Set, prince of the darkness.

Indeed, many of the practices described in this novel are barbaric and savage—not only to us, but also to the sensibilities of Ra-ab and others like him.

Secretly, they have formed a group called "the watchers" or the "eyes of Horus," in reference to a major Egyptian deity. This group, which is dedicated to the overthrow of the system of government and the restoration of enlightened rule in Egypt, slowly builds its influence and size.

Ra-ab and his sister Kiyas are key figures in the revolution. Although they have not yet developed the intuitive powers of their mother, the inner life is very much at the heart of this story—especially in a dramatic confrontation between the priests of light and the priests of darkness.

Eyes of Horus is probably the most mature and exciting of all the Joan Grant "far memories"—novels based on her recollection of her own earlier lives.

Odin on the Yggdrasil,
or World Tree,
Spies the Runes

The Book of Runes
by Ralph Blum

The struggle to relate to the sublime and invisible nature of life is an eternal one for all spiritual aspirants. There are many principles and guidelines which can direct us in this quest, but, unfortunately, we have few "road maps" which can provide *specific* advice about our unique situation and our next step on our spiritual journey.

The Book of Runes is one of the few road maps available to us. It can help us explore our inner life and point out constructive possibilities for action. Like the Tarot and the I Ching, the Runes employ a system of archetypal symbols through which we can tap the wisdom and order of our inner life. By consulting them, we can enrich our understanding of our creative possibilities and how we may be blocking progress.

The Runes are an ancient system of divination whose origin can be traced back to the Germanic tribes of northern Europe. They were last in current use in Iceland during the late Middle Ages. In their time, they served as the I Ching of the Vikings.

The Book of Runes is actually a three-in-one combination: a set of 25 small stones, a bag to hold them, and a small hardbound book by Ralph Blum. In the book, Blum describes the history of the Runes, how to consult them, and how to interpret each of the stones. The stones themselves are thumb-sized, flat pieces of fired clay with a glyph representing the Rune on one side. The opposite side is blank.

Blum has succeeded in reviving an otherwise-lost

system of divination. And he has done so in a refreshing way. Rather than just translating some old text, Blum investigated the Runes *intuitively*, combining his own research with frequent consultations of the I Ching and observation of signs and omens.

As Blum states, the motto of the Runes could be the same as the words carved at the gate of the Oracle at Delphi: *know thyself.* By consulting the Runes, we are put in contact with our inner guidance. The Runes can become, therefore, an oracle, teacher, and friend.

"Consulting the Runes enables us to bypass the strictures of reason, the fetters of conditioning and the momentum of habit. For a brief span of interacting with the Runes you are declaring a free zone in which your life is malleable, vulnerable, open to transformation," writes Blum. In this way, working with the Runes can open a doorway to the exploration of our higher self and our personal Odyssey.

As with the I Ching and the Tarot, simple questions which can be answered "yes" or "no" are not the best to use. It is the *issue* which must be defined, then explored.

One way to test a tool of divination is to ask it about itself. We consulted the Runes with this issue: "What is the best way to use the Runes?" We used a three-stone layout in which the first stone represents the situation as it is; the second the course of action called for; and the third the new situation to evolve.

The response was quite illuminating. For the situation as it is, *Laguz* came up. In reading Blum's commentary, certain phrases seemed to leap out: "This Rune...signals a time for cleansing, for revaluing, reorganizing, realigning...you may be called to study

spiritual matters in readiness for self-transformation."
In other words, the Runes are an excellent guide to
self-discovery and growth.

The second stone, *Sowelu*, described the course of
action called for: "This Rune...embodies the impulse
toward self-realization and indicates the path you
must follow....You must become conscious of your essence—your personal myth—and bring it into form."

The new situation that would evolve was depicted
in the third stone, *Wunjo:* "This Rune is a fruit-bearing
branch....Now you can freely receive blessings....There
is a new clarity which may call for you to renounce
existing plans, ambitions, goals."

The Runes, quite obviously, are telling us that they
are best used to tap into our inner wisdom—the plans
and designs of our soul—so that we can use its guidance and power to transform our thinking and action.

As Blum summarizes it, "Rune casting is high adventure....As we start to make contact with our
Knowing Selves, we will begin to hear messages of
profound beauty and true usefulness."

Job: A Comedy of Justice
by Robert Heinlein

The intense emphasis on suffering as a part of the "religious life" is one of the most bizarre legacies of Judeo-Christian theology. Why would a benevolent God take delight in the hardships of His followers, or even those who reject Him?

In order to answer this question, Robert Heinlein decided to go to the source—the source, in this case, being the book of Job in the Old Testament—and rewrite it in modern terms. This he has done, and the result is a delicious concoction of satire, philosophy, humor, and adventure.

The new Job is a fellow named Alex who is chief fundraiser for a large fundamentalist church. He and his wife Margaret suffer tribulation after tribulation. Each time, just as they are about to triumph over adversity, Yahweh (the God of the Old Testament) changes the rules, and their suffering begins anew.

Finally, Alex makes it to heaven, but has been separated from Margaret. To him, this is as bad as hell, so he demands to go there. In hell, he finds that unlike Yahweh, the Devil does not make his chosen suffer. In fact, it is pretty nice.

This leads to a cosmic confrontation, in which the Devil exposes Yahweh's preoccupation with suffering to the true God, and justice is finally served. In this way, the hypocrisy of fundamentalist and Old Testament theology is exposed, making it clear that God is indeed benevolent and just, not wrathful and bigoted, as the fundamentalists are.

Job is a funny, thought-provoking book.

The Hidden Side of Things
by C.W. Leadbeater

What we see, hear, touch, and smell in the physical plane is only a tiny fragment of God's creation. To live wisely and comprehend fully the nature of life, we must realize that there is a hidden side to reality, as well as an outer, tangible side. This inner side of life—indeed, the vast totality of life—is invisible to most of us. And yet it is often the key which unlocks the door to a true understanding of what is happening to us.

As C.W. Leadbeater puts it in his marvelous book, *The Hidden Side of Things*, it is as though we were people who were examining a huge tapestry in the process of being woven from underneath the loom! From such a perspective, the unfolding tapestry would seem to be nothing but a confused mass of color and ragged threads, utterly lacking in order, beauty, meaning, or purpose. But if we could look at the tapestry from above, and with an understanding of the final design the weaver has in mind, we could see the reason for our confusion lies not in the tapestry, but in our limited, upside-down perspective.

The Hidden Side of Things is written to improve our pespective on life—to help us see life in its totality, not just in its physical aspect. It is a thorough exploration of the psychic dimensions of life and their impact on ordinary daily living, conducted by one of the greatest clairvoyants of the early twentieth century.

Bishop Leadbeater divides his investigation into three parts. The first is devoted to examining the psychic impact of the sun, the planets, our natural surroundings, and the thoughts of others upon us.

The second section explores the many ways in which we influence ourselves psychically—through the thoughts, feelings, and habits that we hold, and the environment we create around us. In the final part, Leadbeater deals with how we influence others psychically.

This is probably the best single volume in print about the influence of psychic energies and conditions on daily life. The Bishop writes from his own clairvoyant observation and experimentation, but with the constant goal of using these psychic insights to help us understand the confusing and mysterious aspects of living.

In writing about the invisible radiations of the sun, for example, Leadbeater shows us how these radiations affect our physical vitality and health. In describing the psychic emanations of physical objects, he examines how a knowledge of these emanations can be used productively, in choosing our personal possessions, making talismans, and so on.

There are several chapters on the ennobling influence of the magnetic emanations at sacred sites, cathedrals, museums, and consecrated places—and the impact of religious ceremonies. These locations and activities, the Bishop explains, exude unseen forces which stimulate the spiritual side of our nature—and can help us purify and enhance our consciousness. His first-hand reports make sense out of many mysterious rituals.

One of the major themes Leadbeater tackles is the subtle way in which we are influenced by other people—and mass consciousness as a whole. In particular, he examines the impact of prejudice, gossip, and deceit in public opinion.

The Bishop's strong statements on these topics might be upsetting to a person who has blandly assumed that his private thoughts are his own business and no one else's. But this is not the case, and Leadbeater clearly articulates the deadly and sometimes disgusting influence that strong negative feelings have on others—as seen clairvoyantly.

Having established this theme, he then expands upon it further, investigating the many ways in which the quality of our thoughts, feelings, and habits affect our own character and state of mind. The Bishop provides much food for thought—and a strong stimulus to discipline our behavior.

The Hidden Side of Things concludes with a thorough investigation of how we influence others—through good works we perform, the way we raise our children, collective thought, and our relationship with other kingdoms of life.

Bishop Leadbeater wrote many books in his lengthy career, and his collected writings represent one of the great sources of knowledge now available on the psychic dimensions of life. *The Hidden Side of Things,* is probably Bishop Leadbeater's crowning achievement in describing the invisible nature of our lives. Every serious student can benefit from reading it.

Lord of the Horizon
by Joan Grant

Ra-ab Hotep is the absolute ruler of one of the 18 provinces of ancient Egypt, but also a man of great wisdom, leadership skills, and humanistic vision. The role he is to play for the benefit of Egypt is an important but unexpected one.

The Pharaoh of his time, Amenemhet, is a friend of Ra-ab Hotep, but has ignored his counsel. As a result, Pharaoh's son has become the object of court intrigue. At last, Amenemhet realizes Senusert will be unfit to rule unless his attitudes and training are drastically altered. He asks Ra-ab Hotep and his wife Meri-osis to take his son into their home and raise him.

The challenge is a great one, because Senusert has been spoiled by those who would use him to their own ends. But Ra-ab Hotep and his wife are equal to the task, and patiently work to help Senusert grow to maturity. They are frequently aided by their psychic abilities, which are highly developed, and by their deep understanding of karmic law and the purposes of human evolution.

Like all Joan Grant books, *Lord of the Horizon* is marvelous reading—a "far memory" of life in ancient Egypt, liberally spiced with powerful insights into reincarnation, psychic experiences, the spiritualization of consciousness, the necessity of opposing evil with wisdom, enlightened leadership in government and religion, and kinship with life.

It is, in fact, the continuation of Ra-ab's life story begun in *Eyes of Horus*—and readers will find it every bit as fascinating and enchanting.